careers un-ltd

YOU ARE
YOU DON'T WANT
YOU'RE
SO WHY

NOT BORING
TO BE BORED
NOT LTD
CHOOSE
A LTD CAREER...?

careers un-ltd

tell me, what is it you plan to do with your
one wild and precious life?

Jonathan Robinson
Carmel McConnell

momentum

www.yourmomentum.com
the stuff that drives you

What is momentum?

Momentum is a completely new publishing philosophy, in print and online, dedicated to giving you more of the information, inspiration and drive to enhance who you are, what you do, and how you do it.

Fusing the changing forces of work, life and technology, momentum will give you the right stuff for a brighter future and set you on the way to being all you can be.

Who needs momentum?

Momentum is for people who want to make things happen in their career and their life, who want to work at something they enjoy and that's worthy of their talent and their time.

Momentum people have values and principles, and question who they are, what they do, and who for. Wherever they work, they want to feel proud of what they do. And they are hungry for information, stimulation, ideas and answers. ...

Momentum online

Visit *www.yourmomentum.com* to be part of the talent community. Here you'll find a full listing of current and future books, an archive of articles by momentum authors, sample chapters and self-assessment tools. While you're there, post your work/life questions to our momentum coaches and sign up to receive free newsletters with even more stuff to drive you.

PEARSON EDUCATION LIMITED

Head Office:
Edinburgh Gate
Harlow CM20 2JE
Tel: +44 (0)1279 623623
Fax: +44 (0)1279 431059

London Office:
128 Long Acre, London WC2E 9AN
Tel: +44 (0)20 7447 2000
Fax: +44 (0)20 7447 2170
Website: www.business-minds.com
www.yourmomentum.com

First published in Great Britain in 2003

The right of Jonathan Robinson and Carmel McConnell to be identified as Author of this Work has been asserted by her in accordance with the Copyright, Designs and Patents Act 1988.

ISBN 1 843 04026 3

British Library Cataloguing in Publication Data
A CIP catalogue record for this book can be obtained from the British Library.

10 9 8 7 6 5 4 3 2 1

Design by Claire Brodmann Book Designs, Lichfield, Staffs.
Typeset by Northern Phototypesetting Co. Ltd, Bolton
Printed and bound in Great Britain by Bookcraft, M dsomer Norton

The Publishers' policy is to use paper manufactured from sustainable forests.

Why shouldn't I work for the NSA? That's a tough one, but I'll give it a shot. Say I'm working at NSA. Somebody puts a code on my desk, something nobody else can break. So I take a shot at it and maybe I break it. And I'm real happy with myself, 'cause I did my job well. But maybe that code was the location of some rebel army in North Africa or the Middle East. Once they have that location, they bomb the village where the rebels were hiding and fifteen hundred people I never had a problem with get killed. Now the politicians are sayin', 'Send in the marines to secure the area' 'cause they don't give a shit. It won't be their kid over there, gettin' shot. Just like it wasn't them when their number was called, 'cause they were pullin' a tour in the National Guard. It'll be some guy from Southie takin' shrapnel in the ass. And he comes home to find that the plant he used to work at got exported to the country he just got back from. And the guy who put the shrapnel in his ass got his old job, 'cause he'll work for fifteen cents a day and no bathroom breaks. Meanwhile my buddy from Southie realizes the only reason he was over there was so we could install a government that would sell us oil at a good price. And of course the oil companies used the skirmish to scare up oil prices so they could turn a quick buck. A cute little ancillary benefit for them but it ain't helping my buddy at two-fifty a gallon. And naturally they're takin' their sweet time bringin' the oil back, and maybe even took the liberty of hiring an alcoholic skipper who likes to drink martinis and play slalom with the icebergs, and it ain't too long 'til he hits one, spills the oil and kills all the sea life in the North Atlantic. So my buddy's out of work and he can't afford to drive, so he's got to walk to the job interviews, which sucks 'cause the shrapnel in his ass is givin' him chronic hemorroids. And meanwhile he's starvin' 'cause every time he tries to get a bite to eat the only blue plate special they're servin' is North Atlantic scrod with Quaker State.

So what do I think? I'm holdin' out for somethin' better.

Will in *Good Will Hunting*

about the authors

Jonathan is a student and fledgling social entrepreneur. He has found himself in disparate and unusual places. Jonathan joined an aid mission to Bosnia during the war; interviewed the Dalai Lama in India; joined anti-corporate globalization protesters in Seattle; dined with the world's corporate elite; made a budget film in West Africa and built community spaces out of waste in Soweto. Together with a bunch of friends Jonathan has recently launched a radical thinktank consultancy www.imago.bz who are opening a political arts centre in London.

Carmel McConnell has spent her whole life being an activist, firstly at the Greenham Common nuclear missile base and latterly as a global corporate consultant.

Her experiences are testament to the fact that you can think big, have a stake in the decision-making process, turn profits and still have principles.

She now works as a consultant, change activist and author. Carmel's major interest is in the link between social justice and big business, and helping large organizations to learn and apply greater social responsibility in the belief that consumer trust is the ultimate market advantage.

Carmel is donating all her royalties from this book to *The Magic Sandwich Project* – a child poverty charity she set up in 2000 to get nutritious food into schools where malnutrition and under-achievement go hand-in-hand.

A percentage of the publisher's profits also go to this cause.

a thank you from Jonathan

This really isn't my book. What I have written is the culmination of thinking and research done by a team at Imago. Lucy Storrs, Alastair Mackenzie, Lindsay Gray, Mark Hodge, Etty Flanagan, Lucy Hinton, Katy Marks, Polly Mclean and Ned Palmer have been indispensable to this project. It belongs to them as much as anyone. Thanks Lucy most of all for your tireless research into un-ltd people before knowing this was going anywhere. We talked to, interrogated and visited pioneers of soul-fulfilling work – thank you all for being so forthcoming with your stories and for being the inspiration of this book. I have had the privilege of engaging the minds of Nick Mayhew and Jay Griffiths – you have made indelible impressions on this book. Carmel thank you for making hours spent trawling through this so entertaining and for imparting so many of your ideas. Rachael and the team at Pearson – your brave faith in this thing blows me away. My parents, Jessica, Amy, Lucy, Ruth, Michelle, Alfy, Katy, Yuill, Kezia, Ninni, Niko, Ranica, Iona and Annanya for special, wild, spontaneous distractions – thank you for making me alive during days of bewildering, sleepless writing.

a thank you from Carmel

This book is dedicated to my un-ltd heroines and heros who have made, or are in the process of making, a successful transition to career fulfilment. Some names include Mick C, Sara, Dave C, Olu, Wendy, Mark P, Sophie, Nick, Merav, Karen D, James F and to Jonathan and Rachael for their support through this project and finally thanks to Catherine with love for her patience and excellent advice.

Author royalties from this book are being donated to Magic Sandwich, www.magicsandwich.co.uk – a child poverty programme – and to www.spaceplc.com – a 'spoof' company that joins but challenges the corporate milkround of universities.

contents

contents

foreword

AT LAST an accessible book about life and how to make it work, from the perspective of an emerging student looking for signposts to a worthwhile future. *Careers un-ltd* thinks outside the box that our Limited world imposes on so many of us in search of a future. Amid new ideas, new technologies, new ways of doing things, this book offers un-ltd ideas for intersecting with unlimited opportunities. Bored with the conventional job hunt? Read this – and good luck!

Jon Snow, *Channel 4 News*

chapter one

---

what deserves you?

'Tell me. What is it you plan to do

with your one wild and precious life?'

Mary Oliver

TELL ME. What is it you plan to do with your one wild and precious life? What is it you plan to do that deserves you? What deserves your sense of humour, your ingenuity, your intelligence, your sense of fun? What deserves your energy and passion for half your waking life?

Whatever it is.

> **Don't let it be ltd.**

> **Make it un-ltd.**

You can do whatever you want to do. You are in control. You don't believe me.

In each career choice comes the decision to be:

1. ltd or
2. un-ltd.

Ltd doctor, Un-ltd doctor,

Ltd underwriter, Un-ltd underwriter,

Ltd social activist, Un-ltd social activist.

Capice?

Cracks are forming in the careers veneer. They reveal a stark disconnection between what it is that we live for and the reality of the work we fill every day with. Ltd ideas of work leave us *careering* all over the place. S Club 7's 'don't stop moving' has permeated the psyche of ltd careers. For in the fear of being left behind, trampled on, or of being overtaken, ltd minds fail to stop and ask the following questions. What's driving us? And where are we going? What are our reasons for getting out of bed in the morning? Does our work match our life's aspirations or are we getting consumed in a daily slog that is hopelessly misaligned from the person we want to be?

Things are not looking good in the world of ltd career options.

'I was trapped in the corporate world by a bravado and fear of expressing what I was really passionate about. Most of the time it was like being forced to wear clothes that I didn't like wearing and which didn't fit me. So every day there I was presented to the world as someone that was not me and everything inside me on an emotional level was screaming.'

Chris Wild, former management consultant

'I do a nine to five day about once every three weeks. The rest of the time I can leave at anywhere between 7.30 and not at all. Whether there's work to do or not. It's all about commitment to the firm and that is measured in the number of hours you are willing to put in. They have a name for it on their six monthly appraisals: resilience. In every appraisal I have had so far there has been some mention of the fact that I like to leave at 5 if I can. It's an unquestionable part of the culture and I seem to be ruffling feathers, if not jeopardizing my career, by resisting it. It's not uncommon to hear partners complaining that they cannot find nannies for 15 hours a day.'   **Sarah Warren**, trainee in a City law firm

'I was frustrated by the lack of client contact and the way I wasn't given the opportunity to apply what I had learnt. I had no responsibility and felt I had walked out of university and into a monkey's job. I left after just 11 months.'

Vicki Povey, Oxford graduate with a Big Five accountancy firm

Disturbing revelations. Yet it would be tempting to dismiss them if this mood had not been substantiated as a national trend. According to an ICM poll covered by the *Observer* those of us who think our working lives have got worse over the last five years are more than double the number who think things have improved. Corporate consultancy People Potential claims the majority of graduates want to leave their first job within two years. Twenty per cent of us rate the experience of going to work as extremely stressful, which helps explain why 12 million of us are now on anti-depressants. Researchers looking at 25-year-olds found them 10 times more likely to be suffering from depression today than 50 years ago. Ltdness isn't working.

This dismal picture portrays the whole idea of work as something stressful, tiresome and dull. Surely not. What we are talking about here is the stuff we fill most of our waking life with. Surely that makes it worthy of something altogether more extraordinary, stimulating and rewarding.

But check this out. By widening our radar screen of possibilities in the world, something quite extraordinary pops into view. It is a quiet un-ltd revolution, led by a disparate bunch of low-flying super heroes. Together they personify a profoundly different conception of work. They are devoting themselves to personifying the change that they want to see in the world. And they're doing it with all the play and creativity they can muster.

You are probably at this moment thinking no doubt they did it with a whopping big inheritance, shed loads of contacts and the resilience of David Beckham. Actually, not. They are no more sorted than you or me. Here are just some of those whose stories litter this book. Richard Reed and two of his mates founded the Innocent brand of fresh-fruit smoothies. Sarah Ratty designs eco-fashion wear for high street brands.

Esther Boulton and her childhood friend founded three Organic London pubs. Rafiq Manji used to trade millions of dollars a day on the stock market before working in corporate social responsibility. Dr Catherine Hewitt works in a medical practice for the homeless. Jamie Rowland was long-term unemployed when a grant from the Princes Trust helped launch his 'Bicycle Doctor' business. Nina Planck, a journalist for *Time* magazine founded a dozen London farmer's markets. Mathew Franklin is using graffiti art to change the landscape and mindscape of Edinburgh's most rundown community.

Careers un-ltd is full of their stories because nothing is so infectious as an example. Nothing feels quite so compelling, gripping or undeniable than a story of someone like us. Anecdotes from someone we can relate to, and empathize with seem powerful beyond measure. For their take on life, the stuff they've done, can't be easily dismissed. They are compelling proof that being un-ltd is possible and that it is bursting with opportunity and adventure.

ltd v. un-ltd

What is ltd? Ltd is sliding into a career because it is easy, safe and secure – even when you know it isn't the best you could do. Ltd is the fear driven rejection of all you could do with your life. Ltd is the compromise without investigation. The giving in without question.

ltd	un-ltd
parroting the boss	being yourself
dumming down and shutting up	devoting yourself to what matters
accepting things the way they are	rethinking basic assumptions
retreating from opportunities	engaging others
single-minded	open-minded
giving up	forever learning
propping up the status quo	changing the rules of the game
planning to do it one day	just doing it
sheltering in the comfort zone	taking risks
working	playing

I don't want to be simplistic – but do you get the idea? Sure, each of these un-ltd characteristics is fraught with subtlety and complexity. And of course there are degrees of un-ltdness, as not all of us are cut out to be risk-everything entre-preneurs. The point is this. Being ltd risks being stuck in a dead-end, dumbed down, fruitless kind of existence. Being un-ltd in your thoughts first is the best way to secure un-ltd career success.

'Work like you don't need the money

        sing like nobody's listening

                love like you've never been hurt

and dance like nobody's watching.'

Satchmo Paige

Dear Future Boss

I am looking forward to finding and working with you because once I have found my way into a good job I will have no further decisions to make about my future. You will tell me how much I deserve to be paid, how much time I can take off, maybe even the colour of my clothes. My future promotion is in your hands and that's right because you are the boss and you know best. I will concentrate on being no trouble to you and, as long as you tell me exactly what to do, it will be my honour to quietly and humbly serve.

I hope to hear from you soon.

Yours

Ltd me

Dear Future Boss

I am looking forward to finding and working with you because you are a business with social as well as commercial objectives and I have ideas I would like to expand in the real world. I would like to learn from you and still have room to be myself. I will want you to let our customers define the value of my contribution, my earnings. You will have to make enough room for my way of being, otherwise I will feel choked and unable to create, as you need me to. I will create a challenge for myself to use each day as a springboard for my success, and, in a while, I will ask you to give me your job, purely on merit.

When shall we meet?

Yours

Un-ltd me

Ltd you is a commodity that is picked up easily because there is lots of supply and less demand. Ltd you is commercially expendable. Un-ltd you is a niche, harder to find, more expensive because it is aware of its value. Which one sounds most like your mindset right now?

who is un-ltd for?

This book is for you if you feel underwhelmed by your ltd career options.

Un-ltd is the equivalent of a career can-opener. Why? Because your happiness and success can be measured in attitude and outcomes. Outcomes you can't always direct. Attitude you can. And one precedes the other.

'Some people I went to school with

are still looking for a job – any job –

never mind the right one.

Right now, the priority is regular money.'

Brian Mitchell, physics graduate

Those sentiments are taken seriously in un-ltd. Many of us have a mountain of debt to climb before arriving at personal solvency. A NatWest survey reveals that debt is a major worry for 40 per cent of graduates. In 2003, graduates are expected to face record student debts. According to the Association of Graduate Recruiters the average student debt is £9,100.

Careers un-ltd isn't just for graduates however, it's for anybody who thinks there may be more to you, your life, your career than you've already got. However old – or young – you are.

If you have no choice but to do a job that isn't a true reflection of your talents, then do that job with an un-ltd mindset. If the only choice is the way you have to think, then choose to think un-ltd. If deadly dull part time is the only thing on offer then do it and do it with an un-ltd mindset. That mindset will lay the path to a truly un-ltd career.

An un-ltd mindset grows un-ltd career options. If you're the junior broker be an un-ltd junior broker. Do it with all you've got. If you're the new recruit in accounts be the un-ltd new recruit in accounts. Do it with all you've got.

Quick! Get a refund if you want . . .

- conventional career guidance

- a step-by-step checklist for how to find a job

- help on how to compromise for money

- top tips on fitting into the corporate mo(u)ld.

Read on if you crave proof that . . .

- another world is possible

- you can be happy, well off and sexy (or any combination of these) without having to settle for a job that doesn't excite

- being yourself is the most important thing

- other people like you have made original career choices and it has worked out – those people share how they did it in these very pages.

why we wrote this book

Jonathan

There is no point trying to hide anything. I am 23. The irony is not lost on me! A student, writing a book that could be construed as imparting advice on life when I've got most of mine still to go.

But the truth is that this isn't my book. Let me explain. I was part of a bunch of friends who left sixth-form college together, all of us disillusioned by the mess the world was in. Before the dome turned the millennium into such a joke, it looked to us like a pretty symbolic moment. A time to ask some really big questions about our values and lifestyles.

So there we were with the guts and naivety of a bunch of 19-year-olds signing contracts with the Royal Festival Hall in London for a major weekend event we wanted to fill with film, music and debate. Behind the scenes, all we had was little more than a pay phone and our student loans. So it was kind of powerful when things came together with contributions from The Dalai Lama, Anita Roddick from The Body Shop and social activists from around the world.

But the event had failed to get to the crux of what soon became the biggest question of all. Everyone around us was complaining about their tedious jobs that were not only sterile and tiresome but ultimately they were stuck working for

companies exacerbating the world's problems. The prospect
of joining this rat race to oblivion scared the hell out of us. We
became transfixed by the question – how can we invent a
career that is thrilling and rewarding while being very much
part of the solution and not the problem in the world?

So we decided to do something slightly naughty and launched
a 'spoof' company 'space plc'. Space plc tours the university
milkround in the footsteps of Shell and Monsanto to open up
a very different kind of space. We did it on a shoestring budget
but managed to lay on elaborate evenings with wine and slick
multi-media presentations. All very corporate, and yet not.
There are felt tips arranged like cutlery and an invitation to
'write, draw, doodle' on the tablecloths. An intriguing advertising campaign has lured each packed room of students along
under mildly false pretences. Moby is the soundtrack to
nervous chatter. Cautiously a common thread of conversation
is spun, a question on everyone's mind . . .

'So what is space?' Nick Mayhew, Chief Executive of space plc.
Bombastic, confident, overly so.

'Space is . . . well. Space is BIG' What? Is he a set up? Raised
eyebrows, awkward laughter.

'Confidence. That's the thing, isn't it? I wonder how confident
you're all feeling: about your prospects, about the future –
about yourselves . . . Maybe some space – for reflection,
exploration, perspective – will help. Naturally I am full of

confidence. It isn't for nothing that I have risen through the ranks at such speed and got to where I am today: Chief Executive. Well educated, a certain poise, good looks, terrific communication skills ... Frankly, I find that confidence comes pretty naturally.' What's this guy on?

'We're on the road to nowhere.' The Chief Executive is ... jogging. Jogging manically to a succession of slides of newspaper clippings predicting everything from global economic meltdown to a sperm count disaster. Is this art?

'The vultures round here don't wait for you to die, just to stop moving.' The Chief Executive stops and looks mournfully at the car advert shimmering on the screen behind him.

It is provoking a reaction. There are scribbles all over the tableclothes. Round-table conversations are consumed with how we might align our values and sense of purpose with the world of work. But, however desirable, not everyone believed that breaking with the status quo is possible. Admittedly Space plc was mooting some pretty bold ideas about being ourselves in a world hell bent on subduing our sense of purpose, possibility and adventure.

'Prove it's possible' was scribbled on a tablecloth. OK, a year later and here it is. The proof. Proof that the life so many of us are craving beyond the limited corporate mo(u)ld is possible. And we've got lots of 'shiny, happy people' to prove it.

So it is this assortment of pioneers to whom this book belongs. It is their wisdom, experience, joys, trials and tribulations that make this book what it is. All I have done is try to string together a narrative. Drawing out defining characteristics of the un-ltd mindset from lots of people who've been embodying it, living it, doing it.

Carmel

And here I am the voice of experience! I spent 10 years as a full-time social activist. I have also spent 12 years within business as a technology manager, a leadership development coach and now as a consultant on corporate social responsibility. I gained my MBA in IT, became a senior manager and had all the benefits of suitdom. However it was my social activist skills that gave me the biggest breaks. Once I knew my stuff and gained confidence I realized it was always best to take action and challenge the status quo – because markets are fast, consumers want honest companies. Now I run the Magic Sandwich child poverty charity and consult on social change. Un-ltdness in action!

I have teamed up with Jonathan to extend my experience as a resource. I hope to encourage you to be true to your un-ltd self.

chapter two

being un-ltd

How's your cash flowing this month?

Still mostly out, thanks. Ebbing, like confidence in that

job with your name on it. It's getting scary.

Un-ltd has a plan. What plan?

PREPARE FOR a 12-point plan to being un-ltd.

It is the condensed wisdom and experience of un-ltd pioneers.

being yourself

'You're all individuals' *Brian*

    'Yes! We're all individuals' *Crowd*

        'You're all different' *Brian*

        'Yes! We are all different' *Crowd*

     'I'm not' *Dissenter*

Monty Python's *Life of Brian*

Rafiq Manji traded hundreds of millions of dollars a day on the global financial markets until one day he attended a lecture on how debt-based economic growth leads to social and environmental breakdown. A rather stark contradiction emerged between what he believed in and the ltd stuff he did every day. He began to resemble a hammer-headed shark, with eyes looking in diametrically opposite directions. One eye was firmly fixed on screens scrolling his million-dollar transactions while the other eye was surveying the fire escape knowing there is an un-ltd world out there.

Not wanting to be hard on the bloke, but for a moment he personified tendencies that more and more of us find a little unpalatable. We find ourselves saying, believing, feeling one thing and doing quite another – often out of sheer necessity.

Rafiq walked out and joined Trucost, a commercial enterprise that provides organizations with a way of measuring and monitoring performance in environmental sustainability. But facing up to contradictions in our lives doesn't always demand such a dramatic switch. What is important here is simply not hiding this stuff anymore. Surely the most profound thing to put in motion is a process of confronting, grappling and playing with these contradictions. That interface when the stuff that drives us collides with our everyday reality is brimming with potential. That creative tension reveals vast amounts about us and is the clue to where we can position ourselves in the future. A bunch of fledgling un-ltd thinkers in the corporate world feel so intrigued by their life's contradictions that they meet regularly for a dinner they call 'hypocrites anonymous'.

Vive la difference! Take off the mask, stop parroting the boss and be true to yourself. Be different. But be wary, for 'being different' is the latest marketing fad in graduate recruitment.

Everyone is frantically asserting that they're different. Don't fear, 'because working at Mars is different', Arthur Andersen has 'a different perspective' and it's obvious with ABN Amro that they're 'clearly different'. Clearly not!

Be yourself. And the differences will be honest, obvious and compelling. Be a true dissenter. Occasionally it gets uncomfortable, but it will make you feel alive and is the most exhilarating place to be.

'To be nobody-but-yourself in a world which is doing its best, night and day, to make you everybody else . . . means to fight the hardest battle which any human being can fight and never stop fighting.'   E E Cummings

▶ Over to Carmel for a view from the world of business.

How business experience reacts

Being yourself is an excellent idea. Yes, your originality is the source of your potential impact. But don't you have to prove you are good before you are allowed to be different? To earn the chance to be the most special person in the latest 50 entrants?

Take the example of Michelle, a bright graduate six months into life with a brand name drinks company. Her good degree, selection centre performance and interview style seemed to ensure a good start to her career. But Michelle was floored by her own fatal flaw — an overattachment to being seen as original. At meetings Michelle explored her new ideas, at length. She e-mailed the MD with a brand concept that she had taken too far and quickly went from bright young thing to a bright young pain.

Most firms still rely on formal structures to produce consistent results. Your breakfast cereal appears at roughly the same price, same supermarket shelf and with the same taste because those who work for the cereal company turn up and do the same type of work day after day. A controlling hierarchy is needed to run both armies and commercial manufacturers, because high-level leadership decisions need to be quickly and reliably turned into

▶

▶ many routine tasks for many willing hands. Factories, regiments, call centres – same principle. Profits are made by consistent performance and repetition of a reliable standard, so organizations need able doers, a few creatives, large numbers of day-to-day problem solvers and people managers. Not acres of Einsteins.

A job in advertising will perhaps allow you more chance to demonstrate your extended imagination than you could get with a haulage company. So if being original is essential to you, research and choose the right kind of environment to form the stepping stones of your career path. Being special isn't always what you were hired for.

devoting yourself to what matters

Martin Luther King didn't say 'I have a strategic plan'. He had a dream and so did the assortment of un-ltd people in this book. Daydream, revel in possibilities, delight in the questions. So what do you stand for? Who do you trust? What would you die for? Even the cover of *Dazed and Confused* warns that 'if you stand for nothing, you'll fall for anything'.

Before we get consumed in throwing ourselves at something, we need to apply our capacity for diagnosing the crux of the problem. Too many ltd people are preoccupied with merely polishing the leaves, blind to what lies at the root of the world's problems. So to be un-ltd is to grapple with underlying causes, patterns and relationships. So, for example, rather than a ltd job tinkering with hospital waiting lists, it's about finding an un-ltd opportunity to tackle the pollution that exacerbates the asthma of 1.5 million children in the first place. Or just this once, rebuff the fleeting thrills of consumer therapy and instead ask the question, what is it that I really live for?

If you manage to pierce the crux of the problem, little, apparently inconsequential, things can make a monumental difference to you and the world. That's the big idea propagated in *The Tipping Point* by Malcolm Gladwell. It is about change, about how little things can make a big difference. It is about how ideas, trends and products sometimes behave just like outbreaks of infectious disease. Malcolm Gladwell calls them social epidemics, because epidemics behave in very unusual and counterintuitive ways. They can blow up and then die out really quickly, and even the smallest change – like one child with a virus – can get them started. Little changes can make a huge difference. That's a little bit counterintuitive. As human beings, we always expect everyday change to happen slowly and steadily, and for there to be some relationship between cause and effect. And when there isn't – when crime drops dramatically in New York for no apparent reason, or when a movie made on a shoestring budget ends up making hundreds of millions of dollars – we're surprised. Gladwell is saying don't be surprised. This is the way social epidemics work.

Devoting ourselves to what matters calls on us to combine dreams of how things could be with the strategy of positioning ourselves on the leverage points. By focusing on the tipping point, any of us could spark a positive 'epidemic'. But going in search of the un-ltd tipping point relies on our capacity for imagination, for believing that another world is possible. What is important here is a sense of vision, but not a master plan for another world. Simply a daydream powerful enough to give us direction. It doesn't matter how fuzzy it is, for the bits that don't have clarity offer us the space to manoeuvre, to be spontaneous and respond to the dynamics of change. Daydream. Being un-ltd involves shutting out the cacophony of background noise. Listen to yourself. Does this feel like the time to discriminate between the dreams and expectations you have and those merely planted in you by others?

If sparking a positive 'epidemic' in your world is sounding a little far-fetched and if I'm sounding naïve for not even acknowledging the need for a comfortable salary then let's talk about money.

There are too many people whose ltd, low-paid nightshift reinforces a sense that they are lucky to have any job at all and they better not risk losing it. If this is your reality, the reasons for going un-ltd couldn't be stronger. An un-ltd mindset instils the confidence that you have more power and possibility for commanding a really good salary, while doing work that you really care about, than you currently acknowledge. In fact devoting yourself to what matters is the best financial move you could make. For in this world of increasing job insecurity, about our only security is the power to find or invent un-ltd work for ourselves. And it is only by devoting ourselves to what matters that we release the passion and initiative to discover or create these opportunities.

how you pay to work

You need to work. Everybody works. Everyone works in order to have at least as much cash coming in as going out (and preferably a bit more). And you have to be able to pay in advance to get cool work, don't you? The chance to work — especially in interesting, well paid careers — depends on how much you can pay.

Let me explain. Your parents ask good friend Mr bank manager to lend you some money to travel. The time in Oz lands you a good job with Quantas. One example of how you have to pay money for cool work. You inherit five grand ▶

▶

from Aunty Sarah, use it for a one year lease on a workshop to start your table design business. Again, you pay money for cool work.

If you can't pay cash, you still have to be able to pay something upfront. They'll accept brains, skills, network or single-minded determination.

What are you offering?

First generation in your family in higher education? Fine, as long as your love of maths turns into a first leading to the courtship of some investment banker. (Er — are you sure you want that?) One example of pay upfront in intellect. No family allies to get you a summer placement at the BBC? Fine, as long as you win the Perrier stand-up awards at the Edinburgh Festival and the Radio 4 talent scout falls for you. Pay in skills. Crap degree and don't know what to do? Fine, as long as your friends need extra paid help on the Brazil 2005 environmental programme (you don't mind Rio do you Ben?) An example of how you pay upfront in network.

Not qualified, not skilled, no money but you are going to make this work if it takes every breath in your body. Eat, sleep and dream the realization of your idea. Pay in deter-mination. No money, no intellect, no skills, no network, no

▶

idea of what to do and no drive to do it with? How then to make an un-ltd career?

Start by saying I've got and can grow at least some of the other qualities. Your first down payment is to yourself to at least identify what you can trade up front with the employment market. Right now, consider what you've got to offer.

rethinking basic assumptions

I shudder at the questions five-year-old me used to ask. They were naïve, probing, positively embarrassing. But the skill of asking uncomfortable questions at that age is breathtaking! And it's something worth hanging on to. Too much in a ltd world goes unquestioned. Any stray questions get dismissed as just how things are. There has been a frame of reference beyond which it is dangerous to go. Not anymore. Our new un-ltd era is beginning to tolerate the questioning mind. And thank God, because the questions we choose to ask, and not to ask, shape who we are. Everything is up for grabs if only we could do it in the spirit of little children, with the questioning mind. We need to find the humility to ask funda-mental questions with little concern for how uncomfortable they are.

'A child-like adult is one who has

given himself a chance of continuing to develop

long after most people have muffled

themselves into a cocoon of

middle age habit and convention.'

Aldous Huxley

Reverting back to the questioning mind requires a level of decluttering, of learning to let go of ltd assumptions, stereotypes and false polarities. Political commentator George Manbiot accuses ltd corporations of colonizing our perceptions. He calls for the 'decolonization of the soul: the essential imaginative process we have to undergo to tackle the powers that have deprived us of ourselves'. This calls on us to let go of the baggage we accumulate during our induction into the ltd establishment. Shaking off the habits and framework of our ltd past is something that Andy Law revels in. He founded St Lukes, an advertising agency that has turned its back on just about every aspect of conventional ltd business. He has 'eschewed conventional hierarchy in favour of the flattest possible organizational layout and the craziest ever decision-making process.' What's more 'all personal computers have been thrown out of the office and have been replaced by public workstations used by anyone at anytime.' OK. That might drive some of us crazy – but it worked for them. St Lukes are one of the most successful ad agencies in the UK, differentiated from others by their ethical approach.

Letting go of assumptions calls on us to start reinventing the very DNA of having an un-ltd career. It means letting go of the ltd false dichotomy of profit v. principles. Letting go of ltd thinking that qualifications are everything in a world of recruitment that increasingly tends to value attitude and personality. Letting go of the ltd, boring notion that time is money, for it denies so much wild, spontaneous, meaningful, fun time. Let go of the ltd assumption that you have to account for every experience as being an asset to your CV. Let go of the idea that doing what you love is something to relegate to your free time. In the beginning change is as much about throwing away and discarding as about pursuing and acquiring anything new. This is all about looking at the world through a new pair of glasses.

Bobby Pugh has been overturning some emotive, awkward assumptions about the stuff people smoke at parties. His curiosity began with a mates random reference to Henry Ford using the substance to not only power a car but build its bodywork and 'that it happened to be a third lighter and five times stronger than the conventional steel'. Bobby's investigation into hemp had begun. But he soon discovered that 'there were no references in any libraries, no books to buy – nothing' – but he wasn't giving up.

'Hemp before the 1939 ban was held in almost the same esteem as water. Hemp was in everything. Clothing, rope and paper was made from hemp as no other fibre provides such strength and longevity. Oil lamps, paint and food relied on the stuff too. This plant has become a symbol of all that is right with the kind of environmentally sustainable future the world so badly needs. Hemp grows well without the use of herbicides and pesticides. The plant suppresses weeds and improves the soil for crop rotation and is therefore well suited for use in organic farming. It is also a valuable renewable resource that can reduce our over reliance on cotton, soybeans, timber and petroleum.'

Bobby's disbelief that this extraordinary crop had been banned propelled him to launch a courageous revival in the use of hemp. Bobby set up the only company in the UK that farms, processes and distributes hemp products. Everything from food, eco-fashion, fabrics, paper, body lotions and household accessories are available online at www.thehemp-shop.com.

Paul Kingsnorth landed himself a job as a researcher for *The Independent*. He figured some Fleet Street experience would be a good idea. But that lasted only 10 months. He admits that 'true, they were useful months. I learned how to research, write to deadlines . . . but they were hell, too'. It was all about 'following the agendas of the other papers; they would be spread out on the floor of the editor's office every morning to help the staff decide what to write. Nothing I considered important was even covered. I had to get out.' Paul is now deputy editor of *The Ecologist*. Printed on the magazine's front cover is the motto 'rethinking basic assumptions'.

'We at *The Ecologist* don't think the world's problems can be solved just by chopping down less trees, building more wind farms or trying to persuade big supermarkets to recycle their carrier bags. We want to encourage people to think about the root causes of our problems. What do we mean by 'development'? What is 'rich' and what is 'poor'? Is technology the solution or the problem? Does world trade make us better off? Is economic growth necessarily a good thing? To most people – certainly to most other magazines, not to mention newspapers – these are radical questions. And that's before we even get to the answers.'

what must work give you?

Out of the following, what is going to get you out of bed in the morning?

When work is . . .

- **cool** – gets a 'really, do you?' reaction in the pub
- **mortgage/rent paying** – you have a room that is reasonably secure
- **a friendfest** – good crack even under stress
- **honouring your purpose** – your soul gets fed too
- **debt repaying** – less than minus £10k on your true bank balance
- **prospect-rich** – it will improve, you train, you travel
- **without ethical degradation** – it's not Enron, or whatever the latest one is.

Alternatively, rather than just picking one answer, put these in order of priority.

being the change you want to see in the world

Simon Parkin was working as a graphic designer for a ltd printers when he was handed a brief to produce some brochures for a medical company.

'In the small print of this brochure I noticed that the product had been tested at Huntingdon Life Science laboratories, Europe's largest animal testing labs, where experiments take place on dogs, cats and monkeys. As a firm believer in animal rights, this was something I was totally against. Alright, it wasn't me or the company I was working for who was testing on the animals; neither was it the medical company. But where, along this long line of product to consumer, does someone take responsibility for their actions? At the end of the day, I thought, it is my graphic design that is helping finance horrific cruelties to animals and I would be fooling myself if I thought any different.'

Simon left and started his own un-ltd business, Sussed Design, which offers an ethical and sustainable graphic design service. Far from being a hindrance, his principles have proved to be a 'unique selling point' – something financial advisors call a USP – as it sets him apart from competitors.

'You must be the change

you wish to see in the world.'

Mahatma Gandhi

To be ltd is to direct your anger at what is wrong in our world at someone else – at the boss, the government, the system. Be un-ltd and try turning that anger on yourself! To be un-ltd is to ask the most radical question of all – what if I am the problem? However pervasive, constraining and infuriating the systems and problems might be – take it personally. Taking it personally means acknowledging the obligation and responsibility on each of us. It is to acknowledge our individual power as change agents. For rather than taking out and releasing all our energy and anger on to some external agent, redirecting it into changing ourselves means that suddenly things get exciting. With each of us trying to personify the change we want to see in the world we become instigators of the butterfly effect. Chaos theory asks, does the flap of a butterfly's wings in Brazil set off a tornado in Texas? Could you and a few mates getting jobs in ethical investment cause a ripple effect that inflicts monumental change on the New York Stock Exchange? It happens.

'Cowardice asks the question, is it safe?

Expediency asks the question, is it politic?

Vanity asks the question, is it popular?

But conscience asks the question, is it right?

And there comes a time when one

must take a position that is neither safe,

nor politic, nor popular, but he must take it

because his conscience tells him it is right.'

Martin Luther King

Un-ltd = control. Ltd = victim.

▶ Over to Carmel again.

Un-ltd control or ltd victimhood?

Becoming responsible gives you the chance to take control.

If you tend to believe that someone else has control over your life – be that your parents, your tutor, the bank manager, the economy, whatever – you will continue to feel that life is out of your control. You might think 'The boss knows best. The Landlord will fix it. I'll see how it goes. My dad made me do it.'

Control or victimhood – what is going on in your head? This exercise will help you find out.

▶

First of all write down five areas of your life where you feel
you are in complete control. These could include choice of
breakfast, choice of town to live in, choice of salary.

1. I have control over..

2. And..

3. And..

4. And..

5. I also have control over ....

Now write down five areas of your life where you feel little
sense of control. These could include choice of breakfast,
choice of town to live in, choice of salary. Yes, that was
deliberate.

1. I have little control over ....

2. Or...

3. Or...

4. Or...

5. I also have little control over...

▶

Why do you feel in control of the areas you have listed in the first part? Consider what that sense of control gives you:

- a feeling of lower stress because you know the available options
- a sense of safety and wellbeing
- confidence in the outcome
- what else?

Now take your second list – areas where you feel out of control. Against each one write the impact that not being in control has on your life. For example feeling out of financial control can make life much more dramatic – will the cash machine spit out notes or chew your card?

Do you see yourself as a career victim, or a person with career un-ltd potential? What if you wrote 'I am in control of' against the answers in the second half? This won't produce instant change, but will give an instant new perspective on something you might have given up on.

finding out who you admire

Someone needs to write the obituary for the ltd supervisor. That anal role of monitoring from on high, dictating orders and reprimanding the smallest slip up. About the only way of sticking out my late-night shift at the motorway service station was to nibble at the trays of caramel shortbreads but vulture eyes not only clamped down on that but held me somehow responsible for the obstinate stains that the industrial dishwasher couldn't hack.

As ltd authoritarian supervisors bite the dust, mentoring is suddenly all the rage. A mentor is a trusted advisor and friend. Someone who imparts their experience to you first hand. Someone to learn from and share experiences with. Someone to make mistakes with. Someone who empathizes with who you are and is not consumed with where they want you to be.

If we were to resurrect the old notion of apprenticeship yet decouple it from the narrow idea of just learning a trade, things could get exciting. Imagine being an un-ltd apprentice at Channel 4 – it wouldn't be about learning a profession, about the ins and outs of carpentry for example, but it would be an experience. An un-ltd experience with insights into the culture of a dynamic profession. An experience full of learning that is transferable; insights and skills that will be assets for life.

And how do you secure an un-ltd 'apprenticeship' at Channel 4? You sod convention, don't waste time with the personnel department. Write to a producer, phone the editor – get noticed! No one is too important, too famous or too busy to approach. What concerns them? How could you help? Temp for them, volunteer if you can make money stretch, do menial stuff, but in the process prove yourself. Ultimately, make yourself indispensable.

'You make zero per cent of the shots you don't take.'

Michael Jordan, US basketball star

engaging others

Practise un-ltd conversations. Do them with your best mate. Do them with the bloke next door who you don't see eye to eye with. Do real conversation. And this is not about whose calls you missed or the invasion of his parking space, un-ltd conversation catches fire, it provokes a reaction.

Being un-ltd can translate as not fitting in. At times, it is prone to being a tad uncomfortable. Meanwhile you're discovering that there is no quick fix, no caesarian operation to speed up the birth of your un-ltd ideas. Put the two together and that sense of isolation, on top of the labour pains from bringing something un-ltd into the world, calls for some serious, vibrant support.

Hence the desire to engage others. The need for a community that will nurture and challenge us. That community can take diverse, kind of post-modern forms. A gang, e-group, boyfriend, tribe or enemy. The point here is that an un-ltd community is no longer constrained by geography, it can take forms that supersede conventional boundaries. Join pioneers of change www.pioneersofchange.net and be part of a global internet community of young social entrepreneurs. Fancy a drink with a community of professionals who claim to give a damn? Then see you at The Princess Louise Pub in Holborn, London anytime after 6pm on the second Wednesday of any month. The same thing happens in Bristol, Bath, Oxford, Peterborough, San Francisco . . .

And the thing about talking with the enemy isn't some casual provocation. In our pursuit of comforting relationships we can't risk being so immersed, so cosy that we become deaf to more profound challenge. Those that disagree with us are not only a reminder of the gulfs in thinking but ultimately they can expose the common ground that is such an essential foundation for change in the world.

Old style ltd networking can leave a nasty aftertaste. But engaging others doesn't have to take the old form of extracting support from and manipulating those who don't share your values. Nor is it about patronizing ltd relation-ships with colleagues further up the ladder. It is much less about performing and everything to do with relationships between peers. It is about inter-dependence, about the mutually giving and receiving of assistance. Look out for synergies.

Coaching isn't limited to the tennis court anymore. The idea has been appropriated by consultants and is now administered in the boardroom. But there is nothing to stop it emigrating to the pub and its techniques informing how we listen to our friends. If we can go beyond the kind of conversation that psychologists describe as level one listening, where attention is primarily on ourselves, then we could have a stab at coaching each other. Co-coaching calls on our capacity for a more intense form of listening, level two, which is devoted entirely to drawing out a friend's motivations, feelings and plans.

being holistic

Being holistic is more than a new-age fad, it's the new un-ltd business culture. It is about the bigger picture. It is about countering specialization and reductionism. Before selling their business to Unilever, Ben and Jerry's Icecream used to revel in it. For Ben, the old ltd way of doing business was about only that which can be quantified, it was 'about profit and loss'. Only if you can count it does it matter.

Apply that ltd mentality to our lives and suddenly all that matters is what grades you got, how much was your starting salary, how big the mortgage is and how many years you have till retirement. So what is your new un-ltd bottom line? Maybe it is the interface between the pursuit of a good salary and things more elusive. This is the stuff that can't be quantified but is inextricably related to our quality of life, it's about relationships, values and community.

Physicist Fritof Capra calls it 'systems thinking'. In our race to become experts and specialists we miss the experience of the whole. We need to reactivate our un-ltd wide-band radar mechanism. Turn on every sense to pick up the clues, value and mystery of the bigger picture.

Meet international genetics scientist May Wan Ho and South London community pioneer May Mo. They operate in very different worlds and yet they share more than names, for they both subscribe to strikingly holistic perspectives. May Wan Ho describes her work as 'no less than a global struggle to reinstate holistic knowledge systems and sustainable ways of life that have been marginalized and destroyed by reduc-tionist western science and technology'. May Mo runs a community food project that 'adopts a holistic approach – tackling social, economic and environmental aspects of food accessibility at a grassroots level'. It delivers practical 'spade to spoon' solutions with multiple layers – 'growing food at the community and household level, accessing economies of scale in the marketplace through Food Co-ops and the devel-opment of individual cookery skills'.

Debates on the rural, urban divide often get stuck with single issues like fox hunting. Judith Whately has dived into the thick of it but only in the hope of persuading the different players to rise above entrenched positions to see the bigger un-ltd picture.

'I am a dialogue facilitator – instigating and enabling dialogue between many disparate groups. My work is based on the need to understand the interconnectedness of issues. I feel that in many cases traditional single issue campaigning is now inappropriate and outdated. I firmly believe this century is about building alliances, finding consensus and common ground rather than remaining in entrenched positions with our polarized views, which leads to fragmented approaches.

'Nowhere was this more striking than with rural issues so I helped launch Rural Futures, which presents a more balanced and integrated approach. Rural Futures is a diverse coalition of nine national farming, environmental and social organizations working together to focus debate on the underlying causes of the "crisis in the countryside" rather than just the surface symptoms. It is funded by a small number of independent charitable trusts. Our aim is to include "all the voices" not just the usual suspects or those who shout the loudest, in the debate about how we use our land. The interconnectedness of countryside issues highlights the need for an integrated and wide-ranging approach. Rural Futures has shown that long-standing divisions such as those between farmers and environmentalists can easily be overcome and replaced with understanding, constructive dialogue and subsequently stronger and more effective campaigning.'

changing the rules of the game

You have the confidence to land a job in the ltd establishment and to set about changing the rules of the game. But how do you work within the ltd system without embodying it? Or colluding with it? How do you take on, play and subvert the system when your prospects of promotion hinge on your very ability to play the game?

Unique opportunities do sporadically emerge from within the ltd corporate world in the form of job descriptions that actively encourage thinking beyond the box. Visionary leadership is often a prerequisite for space to be opened up and nurtured in which far-reaching questions can be asked about a company's culture and core activities. Andy Wales found just that kind of leadership at Interface, a global carpet company. Interface is renowned for pioneering carpet tiles that offer a more resource efficient system for replacing only those tiles that are suffering wear and tear rather than the entire floor.

For Andy 'openness to challenge' is a fundamental prerequisite for any corporation embracing change. That un-ltd culture and sincerity is evident at Interface. Employees are given a mandate 'to agitate, strategize and manage' an ambitious change process. Then comes 'the really difficult bit – how to actually become sustainable – to re-invent products, to source green energy, to search for new materials, to manage the business in a more inclusive way and improve quality of life for all stakeholders.'

The Cooperative Bank's *raison d'être* revolves around an un-ltd ethical policy. That much goes without saying. But keeping change, values and innovation alive requires a team that is permanently questioning, redefining and elaborating on those values while engaging, surveying, screening and auditing a complex array of stakeholders. That team is headed by Gwyneth Brock. While she 'wouldn't be working for any other bank' she considers few companies as being completely off limits as long as employees have a solid sense of values and personal integrity.

Enlightened executives are recruiting un-ltd free thinkers to do the bravest jobs going. These are rare opportunities and there is no mistaking that the job description is a mandate to question, agitate and reinvent the rules of the game. But ltd cultures entrenched in the woodwork of these monumental corporations are hard to liberate. Will, not his real name, came face to face with these constraints at PWC. He helped devise their new strapline 'together we can change the world' – management loved this kind of cosmetic branding. But he is sceptical about PWC's inclination to grapple with the most fundamental questions of all for they risk destabilizing their core operations.

Yet his colleague Fabio Sgargli suggests that the DNA of PWC is being contested in the fallout from the Enron and World

Com scandals. Not least by a group of 120 employees he brought together for a phone conference to tackle how best to resurrect their values at work.

'The trouble with the rat race is that

even if you win you're still a rat.'

Lily Tomlin

Ltd organizations rely on us selling out. Jem Bendell, writer and management consultant had this to say, 'selling out was not only accepted by most of my college contemporaries, it was considered a right-of-passage. If you hadn't "sold out" you hadn't really grown up. Giving a shit about real social issues? That's strange. Worse, it's boring (the ultimate sin in our society, it seems). It's far more interesting to be ironic and read *Hello* or *FHM*. And if you question people's values you're just being nasty or boring. Or both.' Things change. Suddenly being un-ltd, radiating originality and standing for something has never been more of an advantage.

Caring about this stuff is what Innocent smoothies thrive on. Their powerful fusion of incredible smoothies with passionate values seduced the policy makers at Downing Street. So there they were eating biscuits around the table with Tony Blair calling for a shake up in the ltd bureaucracy facing start-ups and promoting a different way to play the game.

Where does this leave you? Well, a few things are clearer now.

Putting on a ltd mask and conforming to expectations is no longer the prerequisite for going corporate. A healthy corporate expects an authentic employee. I don't deny the fun in launching rebellions against the system. But more exciting is to harness all the creative discontent we can muster and direct it at grappling, playing and reinventing the game that we're all so consumed by.

never stop learning

It is fatal to think we've arrived. Destination ltd. Fatal to think we have assimilated all that we need to know, that we've acquired the necessary skills and that life is a downhill doddle from here. Turn off our capacity for new ideas, for absorbing others perspectives, for engaging the creative dynamics of change in the world and we risk going stale. And going stale ruins our capacity to play with new opportunities, spoils any sense of adventure.

To never stop learning is to see ourselves as part of an un-ltd evolutionary process. Not stuck in the grooves of a ltd linear journey. Expect to go off course. Be distracted by intriguing realizations and reflections. For this is about being alive to insights that we can continually reinterpret and apply. Far from being signs of weakness, times of uncertainty, reflection and self-questioning are about the healthiest things we can do to realign our sense of purpose with the stuff we fill every day with.

Back to Gwyneth Brock who heads the ethical policy team at The Cooperative Bank. After college she did a stint at Amnesty International, then joined an inner city task force in South London, before running an advice project for drug users in Trafford. Every career turn was driven by stuff she found exciting yet each move was a deliberate attempt to 'expand my skills mix so that I could offer my next employer more'. But there is a scary thing about ltd skills. Gwyneth has been revelling in learning un-ltd skills that equip her to do the work she loves. But what if our skills aren't aligned with our talents – with the stuff we love doing. If we've spent too long training to be an accountant before discovering a burning untapped talent as a jazz musician the tendency has been to press on regardless. It would be too gutting, risky and embar-rassing having invested so much to then change direction. So we resign ourselves to a ltd life of work devoid of the things we have such talent and passion for.

'Imagination is the most important thing we have.'

Mark Thomas

Un-ltd learning is driven by the imagination. And imagination, said Einstein, is more important than knowledge. Don't let anyone else's shrivelled sense of what is possible censor your aspirations. Remember learning is driven by mistakes too. This idea of legitimate error being a source for new learning is being pedalled by progressive management consultants. HR academic professor Chris Argyris calls it 'double loop learning'. It is about the pursuit of continuous improvement. It happens best when you are free to take risks and make mistakes.

'You cannot solve a problem with the
           same mindset that created it.'   Einstein

A zealous pursuit of learning propelled genetics scientist May Wan Ho as she 'wandered, gypsy-scientist fashion, into many fields of research and enquiry: biochemistry, evolution, developmental biology, rational taxonomy, genetics, and finally the physics of organisms. I longed for knowledge I could live by, emotionally and intellectually, that did not reduce organisms and people into machines and commodities. I learned to love the fruitfly that sacrificed itself over and over again to teach me the most profound lessons in the science of life'.

'*How* I know determines *what* I know.
           It changes the quality and texture, and yes,
                   the meaning of my life.'   May Wan Ho

Greig Robertson was living in Barcelona where the juxtaposition of heavy industry with Gaudi's esoteric, organic architecture sparked an interest in him in ecological design. Back in Scotland Greig invented his own un-ltd learning experience because the plethora of degrees in eco-design didn't exist a decade ago. He went through 'several years of working for builders, then secured a small grant to visit eco-community projects in Scandinavia'. This is just one example of the many forms of life-long learning and education that rely increasingly on our own un-ltd sense of initiative.

Life-long learning is catching on. If only because of the dawning realization that just to stay in the same place now requires continuous training. Doctors and teachers will tell you that much. But it is our ever-expanding sense of possibility, whoever we are, that demands it too. But when our thirst for new experiences and insights into the world surpasses even the most dynamic stuff that goes on in formal education we are left dependent on our sense of initiative. Our ingenuity is being called on to invent our own un-ltd 'learning experiences'. Let's borrow a model for one from a Boston-based corporate consultancy called Generon that is already being tested by young entrepreneurs around the world, www.pioneersofchange.net. It comes in three phases.

A 'learning experience' could start with a period of observation and inquiry. This could be visiting a detention centre for asylum seekers or observing a conference for corporate executives. This stage is about connecting with people and initiatives that are beyond our normal reality. It is often rich in new experiences. So this first stage is an opportunity to look at the world from someone else's perspective. Stage two is characterized by retreat. This is for pondering and reflecting. It is a chance to assimilate any major experiences and revelations. Finally, all attention is on practice, on doing it. On incubating and experimenting with ideas in practice. It is about applying all the learning into a concrete venture.

AGR members want their new recruits to carry on learning

AGR (the Association of Graduate Recruiters) employer members believe that a readiness to learn as an adult is the second most important factor in career success – only bettered by good inter-personal skills. The high value placed on an employee's propensity to undertake training once they have a job is the biggest surprise in a survey undertaken jointly by the *Financial Times* and AGR. We asked top employers to rate the factors that determine how successful a graduate will be in their long-term career. A score of 10 indicates a factor is of extreme importance, a score of 1 indicates the factor is of no importance. A propensity for further training scored a remarkable 8.45 – compared to 5.89, for the quality of the graduate's original degree.

'It is striking that a readiness to learn is becoming a requirement in the workplace,' says John Healey, minister for life-long learning, after seeing the results. 'This is a strong confirmation of the impor-tance of life-long learning policies and particularly the importance of continuous learning in the workplace. 'It suggests that employers believe it is better for an employee to have the ability to learn a language than for them to arrive with the language.' The government is in the process of a £40 million pilot scheme, which will see workers given an entitlement to time off for training and employers paid incentives to take part.

'This shows that getting a job is not necessarily the big career break – it's just the start of the journey,' says Carl Gilleard, chief executive, AGR.

Source: AGR website 13/05/02.

Key un-ltd skills	Questions to ask yourself	Space for you to scribble
Recognize and solve your own problems	Have I ever really solved one of my own problems myself? When? How did I do it? What skills did I use? Can I still use them?	
Translate learning into advantage	What am I really good at? Will my study help me do something I'll still love in 10 years time? How does what I am learning help me get at the best options, career wise?	
Skills on the pitch	What is the summary of what I can offer?	

> If I were to bump into the
> person I most want to
> work with, how could I
> persuade them to give me
> a meeting?
> Could I cope with an early
> bath?

just doing it

Sarah Ratty is a fashion designer whose environmentally conscious clothes hit top sales on trendy London high streets. She is referred to as an oracle by hyper-sensitive trend analysts all over the world. But her brand, Conscious Earthwear, had a fragile beginning. After moving into a new studio there was no money to pay for heating. Yet it inspired Sarah's blockbuster, the duvet coat.

'I was working and it was so cold, but I couldn't stop. I ended up getting pneumonia from sitting in that place. It was really awful. I made the coat because I wanted to just sit inside a duvet.'

In a challenge to the fleeting trends of the ltd fashion industry, who churn out new collections every season and throw away all the old ones, Sarah keeps the models that really work. 'We have got coats and trousers that stay in because they are good, useful, comfortable pieces that people keep asking for. Why stop selling them?'

Sarah's unique un-ltd fashion design philosophy, which embraces everything from hemp linen to a refusal to have garments stitched in far away countries, has been dismissed as naïve. She remembers telling a ltd recruitment agency of her dream to make organic clothes for a mainstream audience. The woman there just cut her off 'fine, fine, that sounds great, but it will never happen.' But it did!

Trusting your intuition is what's important. It worked for Sarah. It also worked for Richard Reed and his two mates who are behind Innocent fresh fruit smoothies. Richard tells me that their 'original business ideas were really rubbish'.

'The first idea was foil underpants and remote-controlled curtains – too futuristic. A bath that filled itself with water at exactly the right temperature – too dangerous, all that water and electricity. We even had a couple of dot.com ideas, but with hindsight, roastchicken.com probably wouldn't have caught on.

Smoothies did seem like a good idea though. Take lots of nice fruit, put enough in a bottle to give you your daily intake of fruit and sell it in shops. People could do themselves some good, and it would taste nice too. We needed to test our theory out. So we bought £500 worth of fruit, turned it into smoothies and sold them from a stall at a little music festival in London. We put up a big sign saying "Do you think we should give up our jobs to make these smoothies?" and put out a bin saying "YES" and a bin saying "NO", then asked people to put the empty bottle in the right bin. At the end of the weekend the "YES" bin was full so we went to work the next day and resigned. From that stage onwards we were setting up the company full time. It took a lot longer than we expected, and we learnt our first lesson; things take four times as long as you think they will.'

A delicate combination of boldness and humility puts the best un-ltd ideas in motion. A certain amount of confidence and guts is required to launch an un-ltd idea and push on when others don't get it. Yet a degree of humility and sensitivity is required to perceive when things really aren't going to work. If your dot.com brainwave www.eskimo-datingagency.com doesn't secure venture capital or if the board vetoes your proposal for the canteen menu to turn fruitarian – a certain determination and resilience is needed to return to the drawing board undefeated. Finding the grit to stick at it, while accepting temporary defeat, is invaluable but damn difficult.

Fear of failure can paralyse even the most compelling of un-ltd ideas. Retreating into a cocoon of the ltd, familiar and mundane becomes all too seductive. Gandhi thought that ends and means should amalgamate. For failure becomes all too real if we are judged purely on ends, on some final outcome. Because lots of ideas never quite make it there. But if we think of our ambitions in terms of an un-ltd process, as a trial of experiments and achievements, then the possibility of failure evaporates.

The irony is this. The best way to overcome fear is by accelerating into it. Hit it head on and dormant faculties are suddenly realized. Anything becomes possible and those fears will begin to look tenuous. If you still need convincing that risks are worth taking – talk to someone much older than you. Their wisdom is often tainted with regrets about not having taken more risks. There are regrets about not pursuing those half-baked ideas that reared their head at intervals through life.

Anna and Tiffany are mates from university. They know what risk tastes like. They founded photovoice which trains groups as diverse as former street children in Vietnam and Bhutanese refugees the skills of photography and documentary film. Photovoice secured funds from the Diana, Princess of Wales Memorial Fund and from grants discovered online at www.dsc.org.uk. Anna admits that it 'would be no use lying'. At times 'we have wanted to throw it all in – to lead normal lives, to be told what to do, to switch off at 5.30 each evening, to not to have to defend our chosen "careers".' But the rewards of their once blind faith and risk taking are 'not just humdrum – they're amazing – because they've grown from nothing. Two weeks before our dissertations had to be handed in, we put together a joint exhibition literally overnight in London. In retrospect it was probably then as we struggled, slightly hysterically, to hang pictures straight at 4 in the morning that photovoice was born.'

'Positive Negatives' was a project working with HIV infected women in the Congo. Celestine was one of them and her words offer Tiffany a sense of resolve.

'I used to think photography was magic, now I am a photographer myself and I can train others in photography. I will never forget this training and what it has done for me. Even if I die tomorrow I die knowing that I have been able to document my life through photography.'

Frank's resolve is tested daily. He is a graffiti artist, working in Edinburgh's depressed Craigmiller Estate, 'just to get this done I have to deal with your drug habit and I have to deal with the fact that your ex-boyfriend is stalking you so you can't always make the meetings we arrange. I have to deal with the dole office putting pressure on you to get a job. Just to get projects moving was such a struggle.'

Reflecting on the joys and privilege of flirting with un-ltd artistic projects around the world Ansuman Biswas declares that 'perhaps I shouldn't be so surprised. It's taken tremendous hard work to get up again and again and again, having fallen on my face and to try to fly again. Conquering self-doubt is the hardest job I've had. Much easier to believe it can't be done. Everyone has a dream of open skies. Who has the courage to jump?'

Lonely, frustrating, difficult times seem so inevitable at some point during an un-ltd project's lifecycle that it begs the question how do you cope? Over to Richard again at Innocent Smoothies:

'We often get asked for advice ourselves and, while we have definitely made mistakes along the way, there have been some things that we have got right from the start. Probably our biggest strength was that as a start-up, we were a team of three who had a diverse range of skills and experience. Having a good team is crucial. The three of us are in awe of anyone that sets up a business by themselves, as it can get lonely, frustrating and downright difficult, especially in the early days when things don't go according to plan. But we had each other's skills and resources to draw upon, and if one of us had a bad day at least one of the others would have some good news to share.'

how do you give your career the best chance in a slow economy?

The key to thriving rather than surviving in the jobs market may depend on just a few simple ideas.

- Slow economy means low risk employers.

- Have some way to differentiate yourself from the many others (about 130k) graduating into the jobs market.

- Go after the work you want rather than hope an advert or offer will appear.

- Use your network to amplify your values as a person as much as your CV as a job-finding tool.

- Be prepared to research what is right for you as a person, rather than take the first job compromise to simply pay bills.

- Be realistic about timescales (everything takes longer than you think).

Put your own happiness near the top of
any list of job requirements.

'being chaordic'

Dee Hock, the founder of Visa, has been making profound comments on the nature of ltd institutions and how they alienate and dishearten the people that are caught up in them. He reckons 'we are experiencing a global epidemic of institutional failure' and picks on the chasm between how ltd institutions profess to function and how they actually do. Hock blames the very structure, the DNA, of our organizations.

In the early days of credit cards, banks dropped millions of unsolicited cards on unsuspecting Americans and within two years, things were in chaos. Dee Hock was given a brief to sort it out. But it became obvious that no bank, nation-state or in fact any existing system could sort it out. Dee Hock was forced to conceive of an entirely different form of organization. He modelled his system for the exchange of monetary value on the complex organization patterns of the rainforest. He founded Visa, an inside-out, decentralized, self-organizing company. He explains that 'the institutions that create its products are, of one and the same time, its owners, its members, its customers, its subjects and its supervisors.' Visa operates on a blend of chaos and order that he termed 'chaordic'.

What happens if we apply this thinking about un-ltd organizations to you and me? Let's have a stab at seeing how it sounds. How does the idea of your life embracing paradox and conflict grab you? Writer on issues of corporate responsibility, Jem Bendell, grapples with these contradictions, finding that conventional dichotomies are riddled with complexity.

'The biggest stress has been my desire not to get swallowed up into the culture of comfortable opposition on the one hand . . . "all companies are crap, it's the system man, its all fascism, we're doomed dude" or comfortable compromise on the other . . . "companies are changing voluntarily and we can reach sustainable development if we just share ideas about how to get there." Mere pontificating and complaining is frustrating – there's stuff we can do now, to fix the worst bits of the mainstream or build just and sustainable alternatives. Doing such stuff is not "comfortable" as you constantly question whether what you're doing is part of the solution or not. That constant questioning is tough, and stressful, but necessary.'

Jem's first job was for WWF. He was 'working in support of the Forest Stewardship Council that WWF had recently set up. I was supporting a group of companies involved in the timber trade, who had committed to work on sourcing all their supplies from sustainably managed forests. Looking back I have mixed emotions, as in recent years targets have slipped and requirements reduced. What are good ideas can slip sideways into becoming potential obstacles to the whole scale change we need. You've got to keep your eye on the big picture while working on a strand of the canvass. I'm not enitrely convinced that WWF are doing this.'

The spotlight is back on you. How do you want to be perceived by others? Like a graceful swan, gliding effortlessly and serenely through life, while hidden underneath your feet are flapping around like crazy trying to win the race and keep everything looking perfect on the surface?

Turn this analogy on its head. Imagine bringing things to the surface, admitting to the world the creative tension in our lives between chaos and order, spontaneity and structure. Andy Law and the team at St Lukes advertising agency behave like upside-down swans 'because the tiny interactions between humans explode daily, the detritus of creative interrogation lies around everywhere and overspills wastepaper baskets, routine discussions and decisions are debated and discarded openly'. Their feet are flapping wildly and playfully in clients' faces every minute of the day. It provides a 'charged, noisy, vibrant and fun atmosphere from which there is little escape'.

But the crux is this, amidst the playful chaos our body underneath is gliding forward. It may not have a destination but it is driven by an open, honest, dynamic process of exploration and not by the theatre of 'I am so sorted'.

Anarchy, raves Andy Law, 'lies deep in the heart of the creative process. I know that chaos is so valuable that ideas produced without it sound hollow and dull.' But it is the interface, the creative tension, that is exciting here. Lose spontaneity and risk being stiff, numb and boring. But let's not resist structure altogether, for that would miss the potential and make us a reckless liability. So somewhere in the midst of constant change and flux, there needs to be an anchor for our attention, values and direction.

playing

In the world of ltd work, what do we mean by play? Hanging a two-foot-long piece of toilet paper from the back of your pants and acting genuinely surprised when someone points it out? Hiding the boss's car at the other end of the car park? Not convinced? Sure play can be idle antics but it's so much more powerful than that. Because play isn't the opposite of work, nor is it leisure and it's certainly not frivolous.

Play is about being alive. Play is freedom, energy, spontaneity. Play is about extracting life, laughter and beauty from the stuff we think of as mundane. Play is flirting with possibility, it is playing at the boundaries. It is the taste of autonomy. Playtime is not for grown-ups, warns the voice of convention. But hey, loosen up, for play is about making the most of life.

Pat Kane, former pop singer and social commentator has called for a new 'play ethic' to replace our obsolete ideas of work. But it's more than just counteracting work and play. Un-ltd players 'understand the core political fact of the knowledge economy: you need my brains, and my heart, and my willingness, more than I need your money and security.'

A boring career

is also an unsuccessful career.

Playing un-ltd sometimes involves deciding not to play other people's games. Gandhi called it non-co-operation, asserting 'we will make you irrelevant to our lives'. If others' purpose, values and games clash violently with our own, we can choose not to play.

Or we can choose to play a different game. There is a bloke who cycled the 12 miles into work in London everyday and chained his bike to some average-looking railings in Marylebone. Then one day a fancy-looking sign appeared prohibiting the parking of bikes. Naturally our cyclist was rather cross, he obeyed the order, but on subsequent days he chained to the railings a kettle, a frying pan, a little action man (on a bike) and an ironing board. Then he created a website www.whatshouldiputonthefence.com that got 200,000 hits and a full-page feature in the *Evening Standard*. And although the landlord of Bentinck Mews, London W1 didn't back down, our cyclist made people smile. And needless to say the council is now on the case with cycle railings.

un-ltd stories

Here is a summary of some un-ltd stories. What's interesting is that each has a turning point in their lives and that they embody a sense of fulfilment that is broader than conventional ideas of success.

Name	Starting point	Turning point	Un-ltd point (now)
Chris Wild	Teacher for a year, then management consultant and group coach.	Spending most of a high powered meeting with an investment bank writing lyrics for a new song. Being taken under the wing of a record producer who was a catalyst for recording his first tracks.	Paying attention to his passion and talent for singing. Developing the confidence to trust his instincts. Turning to his friends for support when deciding to leave his job to pursue a music career.
Sarah Ratty	Irritated that she couldn't buy the clothes she wanted on the high street. Sarah was told by the careers service to give up on dreams of selling eco fashion wear.	Frustration of working for a number of clothes manufacturers who didn't care about their supply chains. She was horrified at the amount of outdated stock that was binned. Sarah started by cutting up the previous season's collections and making patchwork sweaters.	Her company, Conscious Earthwear, supplies high street brands with eco fashion wear made from environmentally sensitive materials and not stitched in far away countries.

Name	Starting point	Turning point	Un-ltd point (now)
Mathew Franklin	Grew up in Dublin and studied visual communications at college.	Moving to Edinburgh. While working in a hotel he checked out an Arts Centre in the run down community of Craigmiller.	Using graffiti to transform the landscape and mindscape of the community. Helping local kids paint murals that raise questions about self-respect. Now his phone never stops ringing and he has to juggle a portfolio of community arts projects.
Dr Catherine Hewitt	GP for 30 years in Stoke on Trent.	Children becoming independent and finding she had more time and fewer responsibilities. It was a gradual process that started with her going part time at the medical practice and volunteering her skills to the homeless at a local soup kitchen.	Starting a medical practice for the homeless and asylum seekers. Doing it with limited resources. Not giving it up when suddenly new premises she thought they'd secured fell through when the neighbours complained about the sort of people she provides a service for.

Name	Starting point	Turning point	Un-ltd point (now)
Rob Lake	Got a degree in French and German and worked as a translator for the European Parliament in Luxemburg. Then volunteered for Friends of the Earth before getting a paid job at their Welsh office. Then worked at Traidcraft.	At Traidcraft he met a lot of people involved with socially responsible investment and decided that would be an interesting place to work. He couldn't see any more NGO jobs that looked very interesting.	Got a job in the city as head of socially responsible investment for Henderson Global Investors. His job is about influencing the social and environmental performance of companies they invest in, like tackling child labour in supply chains.
Jamie Rowland	At age 22, he had been unemployed for six months and was living in Porth in Wales.	Received a loan of £3,000 from the Princes Trust Business Programme. Worked with a mentor to develop a business plan.	Running his 'Bicycle Doctor' business – turnover in the first year was six times more than predicted. He is the star of his community.
Caroline Price	Studied economics at University and landed her first job at the Bank of England.	Deciding she wanted to use her economics background for positive social change. Finding a job that she was passionate about at the New Economics Foundation.	Working on a project called 'plugging the leaks' that is helping limit the drain of money from local communities. She has loved training local people to become experts in how their economies work.

Name	Starting point	Turning point	Un-ltd point (now)
Esther Boulton	Degree in art history. Worked in film and marketing.	A childhood friend persuaded her to help set up an organic pub in London. She was excited about applying her creativity into setting up a business from nothing.	Three years later and she loves the rewards of owning three organic pubs. She is always pushing the limits by applying her principles into making the pubs beacons of social change. She and her business partner, Geetie, were named business women of the year 2000.
Ansuman Biswas	Dropped out of drama at Birmingham University. His dreams had plummeted.	Started messing around with a cheap plywood drum kit. Applied to study music at college, got rejected. Practiced like crazy and got a place a year later.	Travelling around the world as an artist. His projects are as diverse as teaching inner city school kids and flying on a magic carpet in zero gravity with cosmonauts above Moscow.

chapter three

---

another world is possible

UN-LTD THINKING is calling for a revolution in our sense of
what is possible. It is declaring that another world is possible.
Sound implausible? Even the 'masters of the universe' are
talking about a revolution. As a hopeless token gesture to
idealism, I sat dining with the world's elite in San Francisco's
Fairmont Hotel. Irony was dripping from the tablecloths.
Speeches about an end to inequality peppered this most
ostentatious of banquets. But dessert arrived early for the
CEO of Monsanto, whose speech was rudely interrupted as a
custard pie hurtled past security. Dee Hock, founder of Visa,
took to the podium and I scribbled down these words: 'we are
at the very point in time when a 400-year-old age is dying and
another is struggling to be born'.

So there they were, the world's movers and shakers, talking
about an unparalleled metamorphosis of humanity. Bear with
me a second, for there is a useful analogy. Let's trace the
metamorphosis of a caterpillar into a butterfly. A caterpillar's
cocoon grows 'imaginal' cells – essentially the blueprint of a
butterfly. But the caterpillar's immune system tries to stop

them growing. Ultimately, the caterpillar fails and its dying body allows the butterfly to emerge. The thing is, the breakdown of the caterpillar's old structure is a prerequisite for the emergence of the new butterfly.

Apply this analogy to the state of the world and it is kind of revealing. Our world and its established order is disintegrating. Ltd forces are relying on a survival mechanism to preserve the status quo. But 'a 400-year-old-age is dying'. And un-ltd people in this book suggest that another world is struggling to be born.

If the ltd world order is crumbling what does that mean for you? There is no doubting that it is a threat to the ltd mindset. It is a threat to anyone who likes things just the way they are. But it is a monumental opportunity for anyone with an un-ltd mindset. It offers an opportunity for un-ltd pioneers to become sculptors of social reality.

I half tripped over some obscure volcanic stones in the Tate Modern the other day to read pinned to the wall a few words from the guy who'd dumped them there. Joseph Beuys, 'creativity isn't the monopoly of artists'. His idea is that 'everyone is an artist' capable of 'social sculpture'. For social sculputre is about moulding and shaping the world in which we live, crafting our lives to turn passion into creative, meaningful opportunities. Big idea. For if we tap into the qualities of an artist – the capacity for imagination, passion, purpose, creativity and play – our capacity for social change becomes powerful beyond measure.

the un-ltd mindset

However ugly protest got against the World Trade Organisation on the streets of Seattle, it was symbolic stuff, a tipping point for a generation now engaged in 'social sculpture'. I sat there on the frontline with Anita Roddick from The Body Shop feeding me cashew nuts. It felt like conventional ideas of the world were disintegrating around us. Tear gas, rubber bullets and pepper spray left us blinded and convulsing in pain. For Anita the symbolism was irresistible. She talked about it as a 'big window of opportunity'. The status quo had been rattled and destabilized. The architects of our economic system would be forced to ponder alternatives. Doubts were planted in even the most faithful proponents of our ltd world order. Commentators were asking questions that had seemed inconceivable before. But memories of Seattle are fading and for many in that movement the focus has shifted from undermining the system to actively proving that other worlds are possible.

Ltd minds, who are clinging on to the status quo, code-named their operation 'TINA' – There Is No Alternative. 'TATA' is the un-ltd, vociferous response – for There Are Thousands of Alternatives. Prove it? A quiet revolution of social enterprise, evident from the stories in this book, is emerging and proving TATA. These un-ltd pioneers are inherently optimistic. But the critique is still uncompromising. To borrow a metaphor from the ecologist David Suzuki, these pioneers suggest we are 'driving at a brick wall at 100mph with everyone arguing where they want to sit'. The point is this, 'that it doesn't matter who is driving, somebody has got to say for God's sake put the breaks on and turn the wheel.'

Are we changing direction? Is the debate shifting? It used to be stuck with how the rising tide of wealth is propelling a few private yachts while too many rafts are sinking. It feels like debate is now going beyond these questions of who gets what slice of the cake. Some people are up for rethinking entire notions of development. Is this what Tony Blair was talking about in the aftermath of September 11 or was it a well crafted but vacuous sound bite?

'This is a moment to seize. The kaleidoscope has been shaken. The pieces are in flux. Soon they will settle again. Before they do, let us re-order this world around us.'

An un-ltd mindset is about precisely that re-ordering. It is about looking at yourself and the world through a different pair of glasses. After all you cannot solve a problem, said Einstein, with the same mindset that created it. Personalities in this book have taken that advice personally and rejected the ltd mindset.

I want to borrow an idea from Milan Kundera's *The Unbearable Lightness of Being*. He coins the term 'words misunderstood'. Powerful idea. For this is precisely the accusation being levelled at the words we use to understand the world by the bunch of un-ltd people in this book. They view dominant ideas of a career, success or progress as 'words

And imagination is the crux of your un-ltd advantage.

misunderstood'. And they refuse to be constrained by these ltd definitions. It is in essence about imagination. And imagination is the crux of your un-ltd advantage. Success revolves around your capacity to see things not as they are but as they could be.

'You see things as they are, and you ask why?

but I dream things that never were and I ask why not?'

George Bernard Shaw

Take the prevailing idea of 'progress' as an example. The ltd world of business tells us we can buy unlimited happiness by purchasing their products. According to a survey conducted in 2002 and reported in the *Financial Times*, 50 per cent of 15- to 24-year-olds buy products to cheer themselves up. Fifty-eight per cent of those could really not afford to do so. Is this progress? Annual sales of new cars in the UK surged to a record high of 2.45 million in 2001, in the same year vehicle pollution caused 10,000 premature deaths. Is this progress? Despite costing £35 million the domain extention of Tuvalu .tv hasn't gone under yet. But the Pacific island of Tuvalu is going under. For it is being submerged by sea level rises caused by global warming. Evacuation of 11,000 inhabitants is underway. Is this progress?

Over to the pioneers of that quiet un-ltd revolution again. For they are busy actively questioning and redefining 'words misunderstood'. Let's stick with 'progress' as an example. Geetie and Esther have set up three organic pubs in as many years with plans for opening 10 more soon. Is this progress? Rob Lake works for Henderson Global Investors in the City and has helped eradicate child labour from the supply chains of companies he invests in. Is this progress? Martin Simons sets up community time banks that have already traded 47,000 hours of this currency based on time. Is this progress?

I don't mean to polarize different ideas of progress. But it is only by asking a fundamental question like this that we can reveal defective ideas that prop up the ltd mindset. There is no point replacing one dogmatic idea of progress with another, albeit un-ltd, definition. Because the value of the un-ltd mindset is the way it is open to playing and experimenting with divergent ideas. A story of the interaction between a ltd Investment Banker and a Mexican fisherman helps illustrate this need to throw some of our most basic assumptions into question.

A boat docked in a tiny Mexican village. An Investment Banker holidaying in the area complimented the Mexican fisherman on the quality of his fish and asked how long it took him to catch them.

'Not very long,' answered the Mexican.

'Well then, why didn't you stay out longer and catch more?' asked the Investment Banker.

The Mexican explained that his small catch was sufficient to meet his needs and those of his family.

The Investment Banker asked, 'But what do you do with the rest of your time?'

'I sleep late, fish a little, play with my children and take a siesta with my wife. In the evenings, I go into the village to see my friends, have a few drinks, play the guitar and sing a few songs . . . I have a full life.'

The Investment Banker interrupted, 'I have an MBA from Harvard and I can help you! You should start by fishing longer every day. You can then sell the extra fish you catch. With the extra revenue, you can buy a bigger boat. With the extra money the larger boat will bring, you can buy a second one and a third one and so on until you have an entire fleet of trawlers. Instead of selling your fish to a middle man, you can negotiate directly with the processing plants and maybe even open your own plant. You can then leave this little village and move to Mexico City, Los Angeles or even New York City! From there you can direct your huge enterprise.'

'How long would that take?' asked the Mexican.

'Twenty, perhaps twenty-five years,' replied the Banker.

'And after that?'

'Afterwards? That's when it gets really interesting,' answered the Investment Banker, laughing. 'When your business gets really big, you can start selling stocks and make millions!'

'Millions? Really? And after that?'

'After that you'll be able to retire, live in a tiny village near the coast, sleep late, play with your children, catch a few fish, take siestas with your wife and spend your evenings drinking and enjoying your friends.'

chapter four

big pile of proof

HERE ARE 10 stories of down-to-earth heroes, written in their own words. Their ventures and motivations are deeply relevant to our lives! Their fears and setbacks, their intuition and achievements, their sense of humour, adventure and play could, just maybe, teach us a thing or two about an un-ltd life.

Embarking on something new and un-ltd is bound to provoke feelings of self-doubt. But these un-ltd success stories have happened to people who are not so different to you. You can almost reach out and touch them. Their success came in stages, as yours will. Their lack of experience took time to become experience and confidence, as yours will.

It isn't very often that we get the chance to look inside someone's life and ask personal questions. These stories are dispatches from the front-line. They are proof that being un-ltd is not a fairytale scenario. They are the no-frills proof of un-ltdness.

Richard Reed
Innocent Smoothies

Innocent is a little fresh, healthy drinks company set up three years ago by myself, Jon and Adam. We've been friends for over 10 years and always used to talk about how much we would love to start our own company. By the age of 26 we said we should either stop talking about setting up a business or get on with it, so we decided to give it a pop.

Our major goal in the start-up period was to raise some start-up capital, so the first step was to write our business plan. And in writing that plan we were nothing if not thorough. By the end, we had basically written something the size and length of the very first bible, but our diligence paid off and the plan definitely opened some doors for us (or at least the one page summary we sent with the plan did).

While there was a lot of interest in the market, we ended up doing a deal with the first business angel we met – a fantastic guy called Maurice Pinto. Things went well from our first meeting onwards, even though the meeting was not what we had expected at all. We went in with our plan, prepared for a serious grilling about the business. We ended up having a three hour chat about when we were planning on getting married and if we really liked the idea of driving a van round London delivering fruit juice. But Maurice's rationale for that type of interview was straightforward and made a lot of sense – he said that when you're thinking about investing in a start-up company you are essentially investing in the people and their ability to bring their idea to life – so you've got to understand them and test their commitment.

Then we had to choose a name for our drinks. It took a long time but when we got to innocent it felt right. We call our drinks innocent because they are always completely pure, fresh and unadulterated. There is nothing else on the market like them; they are the real thing. In our experience, consumers are becoming increasingly aware of, and dissatisfied with, the fact that the mass majority of food products on the shop shelves today have been tampered with, often to the detriment of the product's taste and nutritional qualities. We simply refuse to take any manufacturing short cuts and use only completely natural ingredients, so you get a completely natural, healthy and delicious drink.

The first 30 months of business have shown that our refusal to compromise over the integrity of our drinks has been absolutely right. Innocent has been voted the best UK Juice Product for the last three years at the Great Taste Awards, and we've been declared the best by practically every review we've entered, including BBC2's *Food and Drink*, *The Sunday Times*, the *Daily Telegraph*, the *Daily Express*, the *Mail on Sunday* and the *Observer*. And we've grown from the three of us working from home to 21 of us at Fruit Towers. We absolutely love it, and we've never been healthier.

Some people ask if it has been a problem that we were all friends before we set up the company. In our experience, being friends has only helped. It has meant that we know each other's strengths and weaknesses; it has meant that we can trust each other completely so no one has to worry about who has got the key to the cash tin and it has meant that we can be brutally honest with each other and not resent it afterwards – something you can only do with very good friends.

As the company continues to grow, the demands on us have changed from setting up a company to running a company, which means a lot of time making sure everyone at Fruit Towers is looked after, and is delivering to the best of their abilities. But we still spend a lot of time on the main thing; looking after our little tasty drinks – trying out new recipes, tasting different kinds of fruit and counting how many seeds you get in a kiwi.

And what's really nice is that we've found there is also time to do some other nice stuff such as tree planting days in inner city schools, giving our spare smoothies each week to the homeless and planting dry land orchards and providing cows for the most rurally impoverished in India. And we're all still friends, which is very important.

Nina Simpson: weapons of sound

Q. So what do you do then?

A. I'm in a band.

Q. Oh, right. Are you a singer or something?

A. No. I play the drums.

Q. Cool. What type of drum kit have you got?

A. Well . . .

At this point the blank stares of disbelief set in as I give my new acquaintance an outline of the complexities of 'tuning' 10 foot lengths of gas pipes, bashing shopping trolleys for the optimum high hat resonance, bending double drainer kithen sinks for maximum onstage stability and the subtleties of chemical bin bass beater construction.

Q. So, you're like that band, um, what are they called? I've seen them on the telly.

A. Stomp?

Q. Yeah, that's them.

Except we're not Stomp, we don't really dance or do the theatricals. We just play bits of rubbish and aim to engage and interact with the audience. Whether that audience is the Glastonbury faithful at 2am in a muddy field, 500 primary school children as part of their project on recycling, 250 corporate executives as part of a teambuilding workshop (where they get the chance to get out of the office and do something real and exhilarating) or three men and a dog at an overly ambitious city centre street festival.

 So what is it exactly that you do?

A. Self-employed junk percussionist performer and workshop leader, with a bit of admin and bookkeeping on the side, finder of missing band members in the minutes before the final call to the stage, wearer of silly outfits (as and when the event dictates), navigator and map reader finding obscure performance locations (usually somewhere in Wiltshire), not to mention placator of over zealous traffic wardens while off-loading the van.

 It sounds wild. Is it really?

A. It is, sales managers dance for the first time in years, children are allowed to make as much noise as they can, teenagers forget trying to be cool and find new skills through collaborative, interactive performance. The rhythm unites them all.

Q. I'd love to do something like that – do you think I could?

A. Yes, just do it. Start your own band, no excuses, have a go!

Q. So, when are you going to get a proper job?

A. I have. I've got the best job in the world!

Ansuman Biswas
Artist

It just fell out of the sky, landed on me and woke me up. A pair of tom-toms. Part of some cheap plywood drum kit in heaven. I still don't know where it came from or why it fell through my window, but I had a sore knee and a new toy.

At the time I was living in a ground floor hutch on the campus of Manchester University. I'd arrived full of fiery dreams and ambitions. I was going to make a difference in the world. I wanted to know everything. But my dreams plummeted out of the sky. They fell exhausted, with molten wings.

I had no idea what I wanted to do in my life, only that I really, really wanted to do it. I was good at writing. Or rather, I'd been praised for it by my teachers. Good at writing? Someone told me that Drama was just like English except you don't sit down. I heard that you could do Drama at university. Not going to university was, of course, never an option for a good Bengali boy. My best friend – brighter and more intense than me – eschewed university altogether, choosing to be an electrician. But his political convictions ran in his blood even more thickly than it did in mine.

Anyway, I ended up after school with a place at Manchester University and spent my gap year in high excitement, savouring every moment of life, preparing myself for study like an athlete preparing for the Olympics. When I got to the stadium it was a crippling anti-climax. I felt like Jack Nicholson in *One Flew Over The Cuckoo's Nest*. I found, in the cloisters, no burning inquiry, no striving for truth. Just complacency and regurgitation. I felt as if I'd been herded into a maximum security sanatorium. Around me I watched people being brainwashed.

I soldiered on, feeling progressively more alienated from academia, filling my head with Zen and the Art of Anarchy. I experimented with extremes of experience, enjoyed feral freedom without focus. That's when the drums fell through my window and landed on me. I just started fiddling around with them and gradually got drawn into music. My extra-curricular activities vastly outweighed a curriculum that seemed irrelevant to me.

Over the next couple of years I went through a tremendous crisis during which I felt like a total failure and yet wondered what, after all, constituted success. It was a classic existential crisis, I suppose. The career options I was widely expected to grasp for – the professional, the corporate, the respectable – seemed boring, if not downright harmful somewhere along the line. I was not prepared to put up with either of those options. Both lead to death. And yet I had a terrible sense that I was wasting my life. I was terribly confused by the mismatch between my ideals and the reality that surrounded me. With hindsight I'm so grateful that I went through this horrible period. Sometimes it takes a vigorous shake to wake you up.

So, I dropped out of university and fought my demons for a while. I discovered the healing power of music and used it to listen for my vocation. I used music to contact my own cultural roots. I decided to attempt another degree, applied to Dartington College of Arts to study Music. I didn't get in because I knew nothing about it, academically. This galvanized me into determined action. I moved back to London, crammed an 'A'-level in music, practised like crazy and applied to college again. This time I succeeded. Then I really started to work. And things just started happening. Meetings, offers and ideas. Opportunities rained like cats and dogs. And I said yes to everything.

As I write this, I look out over the Pacific Ocean. I'm working as an Artist in Residence at the Headlands Centre for the Arts just outside San Francisco, on the wild side of the Golden Gate. Last month I was flying on a magic carpet in zero gravity, accompanied by cosmonauts, in the skies above Star City, Moscow. Days before that I was making sand and wind sculptures on an island in the Aegean Sea. In the last year I have painted with fire on the façade of a Gothic cathedral in France, been on a Buddhist pilgrimage in northern India, sung joiks under the midnight sun in the Arctic Circle, taught inner-city school kids in London, sipped tea with the British Ambassador in Colombia, lived with a dance company in China, partied with pop stars, debated with theoretical physicists, rafted through the Amazonian rainforest and lived in a sealed box for 10 days without light, sound or food. This is my work and I get paid for it.

I am called an artist. Is it a career? Only in hindsight can I see the route. I am simply following my dreams. Sometimes I have to pinch myself to make sure I'm still dreaming. And yes, I am. I have a dream job. It's like a dream that morphs constantly from car to train to plane to bicycle to ship to wisp of smoke to nothing but myself flying free. I'm still wondering what I want to be when I grow up. It's difficult enough to accept that I'm allowed to be anything I want. How much more implausible that I should be given respect and friendship, even money? Simply because I have not been content with being discontented, because I have not been satisfied with separating my job of work from my life's work, because I have been reluctant to participate in harmfulness, because I am trying to be happy?

Only by catching whatever falls out of the sky

have I ever been able to fly.

Rafiq Manji
Trucost

I decided to leave the banking business after 10 years. I was involved in the business of trading the global financial markets, specifically currencies and bonds, on behalf of various global investment banks. This is a much maligned and also much misunderstood business. In essence, my job was to place calculated bets on movements in currencies and interest rates, using the bank's capital as my stake.

While I was playing this game, I became a member of Amnesty International about five years ago and through their magazine I became aware of other issues that were never spoken of in the world I inhabited. I attended some public lectures by the London Human Rights Forum. I learned that we have a debt-based monetary system, which encourages and demands the type of economic growth that we are constantly being sold by government. In order to pay back the interest burden, companies generally just worry about making short term profits because without them they will go bust. This leads to mass manufacture, poor-quality products and 75 per cent of resources returned to the environment within 12 months of harvest or extraction. In essence, the commercial banks, through their ability to create money, are in control of our monetary system and not our governments.

For someone who traded hundreds of millions of dollars a day on the international markets and worked with many highly regarded economists around the world, this was indeed a revelation. Debt-based economic growth leads to social and environmental breakdown.

No sooner had I decided to have six months reading and thinking about this complex issue, than I heard of a new company starting up in the UK. It was called Trucost and it was in the process of developing a new approach to measuring environmental sustainability. It was to be a commercial enterprise, which would provide any organization with a way of measuring and monitoring its ongoing performance in this area.

Trucost has employed a new, innovative and unique approach to the issue of environmental sustainability. Its holistic, systems approach is becoming more evident in other areas now and there is a clear move away from end-of-pipe solutions towards a more preventative and restorative approach to sustainability. Those companies with a weak record of incorporating these ideas, and who are renowned for poor social and environmental records, find it hard to recruit. We need to make it harder!

Will Pouget
Alpha Bar

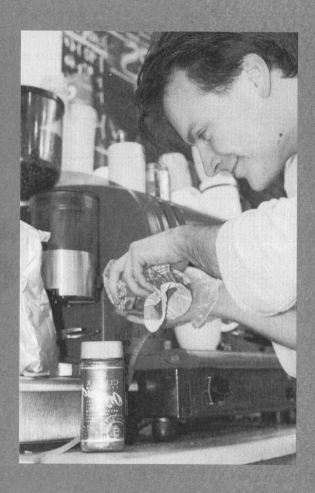

After years of condemning businesses centred on the pursuit of monetary profit at all cost, I began to feel that it should be possible to run a successful business differently.

Multi-national coffee bars had descended on Oxford in their droves. They pushed many independent coffee shops and sandwich bars over the edge. One of them was called Blues. When it shut down I leapt at the opportunity to set up a small student café in Oxford. My concept was supplying healthy, vegetarian, organic, locally grown food that is affordable, delicious, individually tailored and in a convenient 'ready-to-munch' form.

There wasn't much of a business plan. It was just a haphazard process of trial and error. I managed to borrow a bit of money from a family friend. But in order to keep the business financially afloat I had to compromise some of my ideals. Our planet is a living form and I wanted to enhance not destroy it with my business. Over time, as financial stability sets in, I am slowly unfolding more of my ideals and sourcing food from local suppliers, lots of it organic.

Basically the mission was to occupy the smallest possible ecological footprint but also to remain profitable enough to repay loans, invest in necessary equipment and to pay everyone involved! In order to achieve this the operation is very labour intensive. Using our own recipes, formulated to address the nutritional needs of our western generation, far less sugar, dairy and fat, with a vegetarian emphasis, we developed an extensive repertoire of soups, sandwich spreads and fillings, salads, lunch boxes, cakes, snacks and a range of drinks.

This policy of 'making it ourselves' instead of 'buying-it-in' allowed us to be unique in the quality of product offered but also to be affordable, while maintaining sufficient profits. The systems and procedures are constantly being assessed, then refined and adjusted in an effort to find the best way of preparing our products with the minimum of unnecessary cost (both financial and ecological) and the greatest nutritional potential. One result is the virtual elimination of waste within our system, something the catering industry is infamous for.

Our globalized commodity trading system is a bizarrely exotic matrix of unsettling interactions, where 'real' costs are unloaded on to people and the environment in order to maximize monetary profit. I run a sort of ecological 'tax' of increased margins on products that have a big impact like tuna, sushi, coffee, chocolate brownies and non-seasonal or tropical fruit and vegetables. Along similar lines our 'outside catering' activities are being expanded to serve upmarket business clients at a healthy profit while furnishing student or community events with a more wholesome service provided at virtually cost price.

But it has been all-consuming. For two years I have had to devote all my energy to Alpha Bar. So now the business is more secure I dream of travelling to Japan and coming back to it rejuvenated.

Paul Kingsnorth
Deputy editor, *The Ecologist*

My life changed one weekend in 1993, on a hill just outside Winchester. I was a second year student at Oxford University, studying history. Insofar as I had thought in any detail at all about what would happen to me when I left the sheltered environment of the campus, I had my eye on journalism. I liked writing, and I wasn't sure I could do anything else. So I levered my way on to the staff of the student newspaper.

It was there that I heard about what was going on at Twyford Down. The government planned to build a motorway extension right through the middle of an ancient hill fort, some water meadows and a smattering of nature reserves. Local people were up in arms. And up on the Down itself, a new breed of anti-road protesters had gathered and set up camp, promising to do anything in their power to stop the road being built.

I allowed some friends to persuade me to visit Twyford for a weekend; what I saw there blew me away. The landscape to be destroyed was stunning; the case for destroying it was feeble (a saving of 12 minutes on the journey from London to Southampton, if I remember rightly). The protesters were full of passion, conviction and life; the construction firm and their security neanderthals were dead from the neck up. I got dragged into an all-night occupation of the site; bodies versus bulldozers. I got arrested and ended up in a cell. My parents were furious. Parents usually are.

But I lost my eco-virginity at Twyford Down. I turned up a slightly cynical, badly dressed student and left three days later as the blazing-eyed, still badly dressed, greenie I am today.

After that, there was no turning back. I was a convert. I knew now that I could use what skills I had as a writer and journalist for a purpose. To achieve something; to move the world in what I believed to be the right direction. I know many other journalists, but virtually none who really care in any important way about what they write. For most people it's a job; an interesting one, a hard one, maybe even a well paid one. But still a job. For me, it's a (possibly dangerous) obsession. Maybe I need to get out more.

But I understood the difference between the two as soon as I left college. I landed myself a job as a researcher and general dogsbody on the staff of *The Independent* newspaper. I thought some Fleet Street experience would do me good. I lasted 10 months.

I landed up as Deputy Editor of *The Ecologist*, Britain's leading green magazine. It's great here; if you want to write, and you want to campaign for the environment, I don't suppose it gets much better than this.

The Ecologist has been in some important, not to mention satisfying, battles. Over the years we've campaigned against the World Bank, the IMF, the WTO and a long line of governments, individuals, private companies and misfit organizations that we have accused of destroying the environment and peoples' lives. Probably the best-known recent case was in 1999, when thousands of copies of an issue of the magazine devoted to exposing the biotechnology company Monsanto were pulped by our printers, who were terrified of libel action from the company. In the event, we weren't sued. More's the pity.

I've been sent to the Himalayas for a month to put together a cover story about local resistance to the global economy. I took part in the recent anti-globalization demonstrations in Prague. I've interviewed the naturalist David Attenborough and the Booker Prize-winning novelist Arundhati Roy. I've been sent to Colombia to give a talk to the International Federation of Environmental Journalists and appeared on various TV and radio programmes.

I love this job. But a lot of people end up in jobs or career patterns that give them little true satisfaction. It's easily done. It happens to people because, for whatever reason, they haven't looked hard enough for an alternative. But the alternatives are there. You just have to hunt them down. But they are there – and when you find them, it really is worth it.

But they are there – and when you find them, it really is worth it.

Geetie & Esther:
Singhboulton pubs

Geetie and I were childhood friends. Now we own three London organic pubs. Geetie had the idea and was inspired by the original London gastro pubs that combine the elements of good-quality food in an informal and relaxed environment. Adding the organic product seemed like the next logical, if somewhat risky, step.

Geetie worked in catering for 10 years. I studied art history and worked in film, museums and marketing. But it was no longer fulfilling and I jumped at this chance of a huge career change. I got so excited about something we could create, something in our control, something we would set up from nothing.

Geetie decided she wanted to run the business with a partner. She had been seeking advice from my father, Richard, a small-business advisor and, although my dad tried to stop her, she contacted me to see if I was interested. We met at The Lansdowne pub. I had never eaten in a gastro pub before and was immediately inspired by the quality of the food and the relaxed environment. That night Geetie sold her idea to me. From that evening onwards the business partnership began, it was decided there and then that we would open a collection of organic pubs.

We wanted to set up a business that was ethical as well as profitable. We both firmly believe that business has a responsibility to be ethical, to pay people properly and not to exploit the environment. We recycle and reuse everything wherever possible, all our supplies come from small, independent businesses and we use Fairtrade where available. We pay our staff above the industry standard and have a low staff turnover. We only purchase fish caught by sustainable fishing methods and we only use environmentally friendly cleaning products. Even the tampons in the Ladies are organic. All of the food and drink served is certified organic by The Soil Association. We also try to buy seasonal and local produce where available.

We spent six months writing a business plan that detailed every aspect of the business and then raised the money through private investment after being let down at the last minute by Natwest Bank. The Duke of Cambridge finally opened in December 1998. The business has been extremely successful, breaking even after five months of trading and we won the *Time Out* pub of the year award 2000.

When we opened The Duke of Cambridge there was only one organic draft beer available in the UK. We have slowly persuaded small breweries to brew us quality organic ales and lagers. We now have an impressive selection available at the pubs including a stout, various ales and lagers, all of which are brewed in and around London. Change spirals.

Robert Webb
Architect with XCO2

Design is no more than constructive decision making for the future – and that's what I do (with a focus on buildings and cities). Good design is sustainable design. In every design project – whether it's a building or a chair – I try to show how to answer the question 'Can we achieve sustainability?' with a resounding 'Yes, with elegance and joy'.

I started working before I finished college, on the magazine *Ecological Design* and planned a re-launch to engage a commercial audience and very nearly got there. But I was distracted at the last minute by a job offer from a multi-disciplinary team of engineers.

Buildings are responsible for 50 per cent of total energy use, and transport is responsible for a further 25 per cent. If we are going to change, cities and buildings are where we should start. Many of my projects are focused on showing how we can make very low-energy and zero-carbon buildings now, using a combination of good design and new technology. If we can do it all now, why isn't it happening? The answer is simple: inertia. Civilization is like a super tanker taking a very long time to slow down or turn. Change is happening, but slowly. We are starting a revolution.

I spent many years dabbling in other people's ventures. But I am now part of a team that recently launched XCO2. We work in technologies, systems and strategies that reduce carbon dioxide emissions. XCO2 represents the fusion of different professions. Structural engineers in our team do the skeleton of buildings and we do services – the veins and arteries, the invisibles. It enables us to expand and provide a complete service. Thinking in this area has to be more and more inter-disciplinary. The objective is to create a multi-disciplinary design and engineering company that works on building, building components and products within the urban context.

It has taken us a while to establish ourselves so that we can feel relatively comfortable. There are now seven of us – but this is at the end of three years when mainly there were three of us and it was back to one again during a difficult time. It is not easy. And there are still massive frustrations. It is important to be angry, sometimes. Angry about lots of things, about the industry failure to consider whole life costs as opposed to running costs and about simple things like bad management and failure to walk the talk. You get knocked back so many times and you have to sort of go home and sleep it off and come back in the next morning with the same energy.

Make yourself useful – it sounds obvious but most people don't do it.

My advice is don't spend too much time at university. Find out whose work you admire and just get out there and work for them – it's the best way to learn. Make yourself useful – it sounds obvious but most people don't do it.

Jeremy Leggett
Solar Century

I taught the ways and culture of the hunt for oil, I helped to turn out petroleum geologists and petroleum engineers in their hundreds. I remember the hunter's thrill I felt watching smears of oil seeping from the ground. I felt the same thing in a Tokyo office, looking at a possible reservoir on a seismic record or a satellite image. Then there were the hunter's weapons. The drill rigs and down-hole instrument packages probing for the quarry. On top of that were the pipelines and the super tankers carrying the object of the hunt to market – via oil refineries, those most complex of Meccano constructs – where finally, of course, the prize could be burned: in engines, all kinds of fascinating engines. At the time I loved it all. I was a young academic in an industry focused university, surrounded by oil megastars.

So why then the impetus to change? I was terrified about global warming and could see that I was directly fuelling the process; my contribution was turning out well moulded, oil-hungry earth scientists, the mindless technicians of the oil industry. The news about global warming became impossible to ignore. I felt my sense of mission, future and professional identity eroding with every news report that I read.

Soon the fault lines growing by increments in my sense of professional identity reached failure point. One day in early 1989, I stood in front of a class of 40 undergraduates giving a lecture on an oilfield in California. I had an interesting hunter's tale to tell that morning: how the oil had been trapped below ground over millions of years; how Chevron had discovered the monster oil field long after many oil companies had concluded there was nothing there and the technical tricks that they had used; the industrial espionage they had had to evade from their sister companies in order to keep the discovery secret until they had brought up as much as they could of the rest of the oil field. The rows of young people sat listening quietly. And as I stared down at the upturned faces, I suddenly felt that I could not go on. That day, the tensions between my growing environmental concerns and my job description in the Royal School of Mines came to a head. I went straight back to my office and turned to the job pages in *New Scientist* magazine.

In the adverts section of *New Scientist* I found that Greenpeace needed a scientist. The issues were becoming increasingly complex, they said. The penalties for technical errors were becoming increasingly severe for environmental groups. Credibility was all. Greenpeace offered me a chance of moving from one of the most conservative universities in the world to one of the most radical environmental groups. I jumped at it.

Six years later and I have set up Solar Century. There's no company quite like us. We are in the business of seeking profits for a purpose. There is a team of 30 staff and we're growing fast. We aim to help reduce global climate change and to help meet the growing global energy demands sustainably. So why are we not going to turn into something like Nike, which was once small and sweet and is now a transnational with problems? We intend to build a brand that is firmly rooted in social and ecological imperatives. Value will be its immutability.

Too many people are defending ruinous carbon technologies. I'm certain we're on the edge of a clean energy revolution. It's not controversial to say that the wave is coming, just a question of when. Take the surfing analogy – we've built something, don't know when the wave is coming but we have to be ready to get on it the moment it does.

I learned to surround myself with brilliant people who know about business and just do it. I needed people with masses of experience in finance and marketing as well as experienced solar engineers. The finance came from one of my adversaries! When I was at Greenpeace I was locked in combat with the bloke who founded the World Business Council for Sustainable Development. But there was a healthy respect for each other that ultimately led to him offering me an investment.

It has been fairly smooth sailing with the finance. I think we have been very lucky with that. But the entrepreneurial road is a rocky one. It is a roller coaster ride of setbacks and steps forwards. We've had real difficulties with our core operation of marrying up two disparate industries. One is the solar industry, which is youthful and in many ways immature, and the building industry, which is very fixed in its ways and very resistant to change. The interface between these two is tricky territory.

Renee Eliott
Planet Organic

I was moving from the US to England to get to know an Englishman I had met on a night bus on Lower Regent Street in London while on holiday the previous year. I had just graduated with an English major and a Nutrition minor, without any idea of where I was heading.

I ended up writing for *WINE* magazine and worked as a journalist, events organizer, sales representative and professional taster. Eventually I married the man I met on the bus. Then got a job working for Wild Oats, the largest health food store in the country. I loved it and for the first time in my life I knew that I was in the right place doing the right thing. I loved the food on the shelves and working as part of a team towards something. Excellent food, optimum nutrition and sustainable agriculture became my mission. I became manager after three months and then ran the store for two years, learning about natural and organic food and developing relationships with suppliers. In early 1994, I decided that it was time to leave Wild Oats and take the leap of faith to set up my own business. I was turning 30 later that year and felt it was now or never.

So I set up Planet Organic – the UK's first organic and natural supermarket. I wanted what I saw as a more female business that embraced its people, had values and had fun. I started working full time on the business in October 1994 after completing the Business Enterprise Start-up Scheme, which taught me what a profit and loss account was and how to write a business plan. Sure, I was scared. My husband, Brian, and I invested our life's savings, which although not much, was all that we had. I wanted Brian to work with me, but we needed the income from his salary, so I ended up choosing a business partner who could contribute the capital to get us started.

The first Planet Organic opened a year later on Westbourne Grove, London, on November 4. The first couple of months were hard. We didn't get the media coverage that we thought would naturally follow such a great idea and we didn't get the customers either. By December I was really worried with bills coming in and not much money in the bank. We hired a PR company to secure editorial for us, as I was against advertising, and worked seven days a week and long hours. In February, the first BSE scare hit England and people started to come in for our organic meat. Then they starting shopping in the rest of the store. Shortly after that the PR machine kicked in and sales started to climb.

Two years later, in November 1997, when we were doing quite well, my business partner decided to try to remove me from the company on spurious grounds. We were in litigation for 14 months, followed by a 10-day trial in the High Courts. I won the case, and was awarded my legal costs and the right to buy him out. With no partner in the business, I persuaded Brian to come and work with me. We spent the next year raising new money to buy out my ex-partner and trying to stabilize the company, which had suffered during the dispute. Then we took the business forward again.

In June 2000 we opened our second store in Torrington Place, off Tottenham Court Road. We published our first three Planet Organic books in October 2000 and we have twice won the Organic Food Awards Retailer of the Year.

I think I've refined a pretty good strategy for negotiating my way over hurdles and intensely testing moments. If I've learned anything, I've learned that there is and needs to be constant change in business and life. To handle that within a company, you must have a core ideology, a values statement against which decisions can be measured to give the company purpose and its people vision. This must stay constant in the midst of changing management, people, markets and trends. Our values statement is as follows: to provide organic and natural products that you can trust; to promote healthier living in the community; to create a shopping experience that's fun, educational and rewarding; to conduct our business in a fair, honest and responsible way and to respect our employees, customers, suppliers and advisors.

To handle change personally – which can be and has been intensely testing – my belief is integrity and dignity at all times and that, above all, you must trust. When faced with seemingly insurmountable hurdles I have done my best, allowed the process to unfold, trusted that I (and the company) will be okay and taken excellent care of myself – eating well, getting enough rest and sleep, exercising and meditating. I know this sounds clichéd, but in times of stress it's all too easy to indulge in that extra glass of wine, eat badly and forget about the gym. You must look after yourself particularly well at these times so that you are clear and focused, and best able to handle the obstacles and challenges that arise in business and life. I take support from friends and family, but do not clutter the situation with too many people, as you can be pulled apart by well meaning people imparting their personal wisdom or views on a problem. It can be very confusing to hear what *everyone else* thinks you should do about something. It's better to determine what you really want and then focus on it completely. If you know what you want, you can go out and get it.

What is most important, however, is to know yourself. Know your strengths and weaknesses. Surround yourself with people who are skilled where you are not. Be honest with yourself. Trust your instincts and intuition. And take those leaps of faith that are terrifying, but that catapult you forward. The trapeze artist must let go of the trapeze before they can grab hold of the approaching trapeze. Make the leap, forge your own path and trust in the process.

Make the leap, forge your own path and trust in the process

proof analysis

A number of the stories given above show that it is possible to build an un-ltd career around a socially responsible enterprise. These pioneers have found ways to raise finance – you really don't have to be rich to be a social entrepreneur. Social enterprise has a different playing field from ltd business, it is free of the old boys network and the usual impediments to securing finance. This view is supported by Social Enterprise London, an umbrella group with an advice service.

Q. *Carmel:* **Do you have to be rich to start a social enterprise?**

A. *Robin Harris, Social Enterprise London:* No you don't have to be rich. There are several funding opportunities for social enterprises, particularly from Community Development Finance Initiatives. Just to give you an idea of accessible finance for social enterprise – Great London Enterprise www.gle.co.uk, London Rebuilding Society, www.londonrebuilding.com, Industrial Common Ownership Finance www.icof.co.uk, Local Investment Fund www.bitc.org.uk and London Development Agency www.lda.gov.uk.

> The whole business ethic of social enterprise means that there is a concerted effort to move away from grant dependency towards self-sustainability, hence the concentration on loan options. (The 'rough guide to being un-ltd' section is packed with many more funding leads available around the UK.)

What follows is a look at three individual's own perspectives on the key changes they made in their lives – people we've already met in this chapter. We have seen that their eventual success resulted from a certain dissatisfaction with their personal status quo. This led them to take some action – which at the time felt pretty uncomfortable. The starting and turning points in their journeys, plus details of the direct action they took and how they measure their success today, have been highlighted in a table. While you read through it consider and perhaps reflect on what might be happening in your own life and what a turning point might look like for you.

Name	Starting point	Turning point	Direct action	Un-ltd success measures
Ansuman Biswas, Artist	Student at Manchester University. Bengali background.	I had a terrible sense that I was wasting my life. I was terribly confused by the mismatch between my ideals and the reality that surrounded me (at university).	I discovered the healing power of music and used it to listen for my vocation. I used music to contact my own cultural roots. I decided to attempt another degree, applied to Dartington College of Arts to study Music. I didn't get in . . . so I crammed an 'A'-level in music, practised like crazy and applied to college again. This time I succeeded. Then I really started to work. And things just started happening.	As I write this, I look out over the Pacific Ocean. I'm working as an Artist in Residence at the Headlands Centre for the Arts just outside San Francisco. I am called an artist. Is it a career? Only in hindsight can I see the route. I am simply following my dreams. Sometimes I have to pinch myself to make sure I'm still dreaming. And yes, I am. I have a dream job.

Name	Starting point	Turning point	Direct action	Un-ltd success measures
Rafiq Manji, Economist	I worked in banking for 10 years. I was involved in the business of trading the global financial markets, specifically currencies and bonds on behalf of various global investment banks.	I became a member of Amnesty International . . . and became aware of other issues that were never spoken of in the world I inhabited. I attended some public lectures by the London Human Rights Forum and learned that debt-based economic growth leads to social and environmental breakdown.	Working within the system, I felt I had a better understanding of how it worked than those on the outside who were working to change it. In the end, I felt it was worth trying to at least think about ways of changing the system and I certainly needed a break from it. I heard of a new company starting up in the UK. It was called Trucost. It was to be a commercial enterprise, which would provide any organization with a way of measuring and monitoring its ongoing performance in this area.	I joined Trucost back in April 2000 and have been amazed at the interest in this area.

Name	Starting point	Turning point	Direct action	Un-ltd success measures
Paul Kingsnorth, Journalist	I was a second year student at Oxford University, studying history.	As a reporter for the student newspaper I lost my eco-virginity at Twyford Down. I turned up a slightly cynical, badly dressed student and left three days later as the blazing-eyed, still badly dressed, greenie I am today. It was the first of the many road protests that came to define the environmental movement of the 1990s.	I landed myself a job as a researcher and general dogsbody on the staff of *The Independent* newspaper. They were useful months; I learned how to research, write to deadlines, etc, etc. But they were hell, too. I left and went through jobs at environmental groups and as a freelance journalist until I ended up where I am now, as Deputy Editor of *The Ecologist*, Britain's leading green magazine.	It's great here; if you want to write, and you want to campaign for the environment, I don't suppose it gets much better than this.

I've been sent to the Himalayas for a month to put together a cover story about local resistance to the global economy. I've interviewed the naturalist David Attenborough and the Booker Prize-winning novelist Arundhati Roy. |

chapter five

a rough guide to being un-ltd

ENTRENCHED IN a ltd corporation? Stifled by managers with MBAs in dumbing down your sense of possibility in the world? Or maybe you've just graduated? Your student loan flitted away long ago. You are at the overdraft limit and the bank is closing in on you with deadlines and APRs and it's looking a bit scary. The impending culture shock of joining the rat race haunts you.

No wonder you've got un-ltd on the brain. You're convinced, impatient. But what to do? Where to go? You need that final bit of proof. You need down-to-earth, practical stuff on how to be un-ltd. Maybe you need a 'rough guide'.

What follows is a rough guide that tackles the world of un-ltd work with a strong sense of adventure. This is not a definite, comprehensive a to z of anything. Nor does it treat life as a pursuit of the ultimate career destination. It is a handbook in how to navigate a journey rich in experiences. It is a whirlwind tour of un-ltd possibilities.

climate

Un-ltd minds look beyond a fleeting fashion craze to ask, in the context of what is important in the world, what's hot and what's not? For what's not so hot, recall that fickle whirlwind of dot.com hype and hysteria that made such a bungled entry into the new millennium. Frivolous entrepreneurs lost everything. Internet prodigy boo.com collapsed, as did countless others. On the eve of the millennium Boo was destined to be worth $1 billion, three months later it had gone. Does Enron indicate that monumental corporations are heading for the same fate? Its collapse has led to 'the biggest destruction of stock market wealth on record' (*Guardian Finance*, 8 June 2002). Enron symbolizes the end of a particularly arrogant way of managing large organizations and the start of more transparent and trust-based financial cultures. But never mind the corruption, the stifling scale and bureaucracy of trans-national corporations is losing initiative rich graduates, who are being engaged instead by small dynamic enterprises. Multi-nationals have joined dot.bombs as the decidedly tired emblems of an era being superseded by something altogether more exciting.

Social enterprise is emerging as a brave new economy. Social enterprise represents a challenge to old dichotomies that polarized the charity and business worlds. They are positioned somewhere between and beyond the conventional private and public sectors. They are businesses that bring to social problems the same enterprise and imagination that conventional entrepreneurs bring to getting rich. Social enterprises are competitive businesses that are driven by the interests of the community and the environment. They have governance and ownership structures that revolve around the people they affect. The government has just appointed a Minister for Social Enterprise who comes with a task force on removing impediments to this quiet revolution.

Social enterprise is the epitome of the un-ltd mindset. The people within it are doing what they love and are applying all the creativity and imagination they can muster to furthering a social purpose. Greenwich Leisure is an innovative employee-owned 'Leisure Trust' that manages 26 public leisure centres, listed at www.gll.org.uk. It is a community-based business passionate about the staff reflecting the ethnic diversity of the community, about partnership, about profit being reinvested in staff training and about a culture of continuous improvement.

Artist Paul Monks was working in a studio space lent to him by Hackney psychiatric hospital. His studio became a haven for artistic expression, as curious patients seeking refuge from the monotony of life on the psychiatric ward, immersed themselves in a world of paint and colour. Paul found this latent artistic talent too compelling to ignore. He set up a project, www.corearts.co.uk, to harness that creativity. It offers therapeutic forms of expression that enhance self-esteem and creates artistic products to sell, exhibit, broadcast and perform. Core Arts is sustained by a combination of sporadic grants from the likes of www.tudortrust.org.uk and www.sel.org.uk along with more predictable revenue generated by print and design work.

Social enterprises are debunking myths about the unemployment and decay of inner cities pedalled by the ltd establishment. Tower Hamlets, the country's most deprived borough, has four times as many businesses per resident than Sunderland. Gordon Brown has just trumpeted the 'Inner City 100', the top one hundred fastest-growing companies in the country's most deprived areas; more details can be seen at www.innercity100.org.uk. Enterprises as diverse as technology consultants TechnoPhobia and Manchester-based property developers Urban Splash are busy exploiting and fostering the creativity of the 'inner city buzz'.

currency

Popular wisdom has it that there's an inverse relationship between the public utility and value of your work and the amount you get paid. Not entirely the case, according to the personalities that litter this book. But needless to say, doing the un-ltd thing of being driven by your values does come into conflict with the most ostentatious of ltd incomes and lifestyles. According to *Business Week,* Disney's Michael Eisner makes $17,348 an hour and that's frankly obscene.

---

what do graduates earn?

In 2001 243,000 graduates left UK universities. Of those, 130,000 had a first or 2:1.

Expected average graduate salaries of £18,700 for those starting work in 2002 have only risen by 1 per cent compared with expectations in 2001. This very modest increase compares with annual rises in expected salaries of between 6 per cent and 10 per cent each year for the previous six years, again suggesting that this year's crop of graduates are much less confident about their job prospects.

Source: Association of Graduate Recruiters

A career that doesn't repeatedly open your heart and mind may be the worst investment decision you ever make. Don't be surprised if being un-ltd reaps financial rewards that surpass the pay cheque of ltd jobs. How? By giving you a career that you care about, that allows you to perform with your heart and soul and not just brain. The point is this. Un-ltd careers can be valued in the currencies of more than just money. Measure your un-ltd work in the currency of laughter, fulfilment and sense of purpose and you'll break the scales on the financial barometers. Of course you can't forget the mortgage repayments, but to forget about the currencies of humour, ingenuity, passion and fun will leave you emotionally and morally bankrupt.

Getting your hands on cash because your debts are only getting worse or because now feels like the time to buy a house sounds like an imperative. But going for short-term cash in an area of work that isn't fulfilling and sustaining is going to be an expensive choice. Why? Because if you land a job you don't enjoy, it is kind of easy to indulge in buying superfluous stuff and in expensive pleasures as escapism from the soul-destroying day job.

Consider what your true living costs are. Consider what you really need to spend. Ask yourself, are you willing to invest in finding the thing that is most you. Richard Branson did it by leaving school and starting a magazine he called *Student*. If you find a way to do the work that means the most to you – you'll give it all you've got and over time money will sort itself out. And a bunch of other currencies, such as a sense of self worth, of challenge, of continued learning, of creative joy stack up to a currency that can only come with an un-ltd career.

Prepare for a dose of un-ltd financial advice. You could well be struggling, particularly if you are in one of four scenarios –

if you are trying to sustain yourself through further study, if you are working freelance, if you are setting up a new enterprise or if you are currently unemployed. Let's tackle each scenario in turn.

studying

If juggling three jobs just to pay for a course is causing burnout, take out a Career Development Loan. The Department for Education and Skills is providing no-interest career development loans of up to £8,000 through The Cooperative Bank, www.co-operativebank.co.uk. If you are studying for a degree you've probably already checked out the student loans company on www.slc.co.uk but if you're planning to do another degree there is funding and scholarship information at www.postgrad.hobsons.com.

going freelance

Go self-employed and you join a community of freelance professionals that has grown by a startling 300 per cent over the last two decades. But working freelance comes with a warning about planning for the boom–bust nature of personal finances as lucrative projects come and go. *Free Agent Manual* by Josephine Monroe is packed with the tools indispensable to those rejecting ideas of a long-serving corporate life in favour of becoming a self-employed 'free agent'.

Take the experience of freelance musician Ysanne Spevack, 'I played for the Queen and the other queen, Elton John, but the Spice Girls were there and it felt like I should have swapped places.' Ysanne's music interests now include composing soundtracks for Channel 4 but they haven't always been so lucrative. She has juggled a portfolio career that included a three-days-a-week marketing job for www.organicsdirect.co.uk to sustain the early days of her music career.

setting up a new enterprise

If your entrepreneurial spirit finds you up against the reality of launching and sustaining a new venture, money can be a real test. Beginnings are notoriously hard. *The Beermat Entrepreneur* is a top selling guide for turning the idea you scrawled on a beermat into a thriving business – see www.beermatentrepreneur.com. If you need a bank loan try www.triodos.co.uk, which lends to ventures as diverse as local farms and micro-credit in developing countries. For capital to rejuvenate old properties target The Ecology Building Society – www.ecology.co.uk. NatWest have a fund for community investment or, for a bank designed entirely for the social economy, check out www.unity-uk.com. The Cooperative Bank's ethical stance makes it an attractive place to visit on the high street. The UK Social Investment Forum website www.uksif.org is rich with leads on investment, ranging from www.henderson.com who have over £1 billion of funds

with an ethical brief to the independent financial advisors
www.ethicalmoney.org whose offices are dotted around the UK.

Suddenly everyone is giving awards for innovative social
ventures and they come with valuable chunks of investment.
Upstarts Awards have been launched to reveal and support
the stars of social enterprise. To find out more about being
awarded £15,000 check out www.upstarts.org.uk. And for the
perfect un-ltd funding opportunity log on to www.unltd.org.uk
for grants of £2,500 being awarded to social entrepreneurs
with a promising idea and £10,500 to ventures that seek the
investment to expand.

unemployed

If you find yourself unemployed, you probably can't escape
hearing about the New Deal – www.newdeal.gov.uk. But part of the
package offers you support in developing a business plan and
securing finance along with funds to pay for training. To inves-
tigate modern apprenticeships check out www.realwork
realpay.info. The Princes Trust provides low-interest loans, small
grants and a mentoring service to 18-30 years-old with a good
idea for a new business. Their programmes have helped launch
47,000 businesses and are targeted at those who would
otherwise struggle to get started – see www.princes-trust.org.uk.
Jamie Rowland, from Porth in Wales, was 22 and had been
unemployed for six months when he received a loan of £3,000

from the Princes Trust Business Programme. He set up his 'Bicycle Doctor' business and turnover in the first year was £100,000 against his forecast of £15,000. While 'starting the business has not made me rich, it has given me more satisfaction than any amount of money could bring'.

culture shock

'Low trust' ltd cultures still mar too many people's experience of work. Does your ltd workplace value compliance over innovation, hierarchy over teams, secrecy over transparency, homogeneity over diversity and conformity over risk taking? Risk going on the offensive and try propagating a more un-ltd mindset. A couple of books might come in handy. A dip into *Change Activist* by Carmel McConnell will give you the impetus to apply the more effective principles of a social activist in your workplace. *Feel the Fear and Do it Anyway* by Susan Jeffers has helped millions overcome some of their deepest fears.

> Does your ltd workplace value compliance over innovation, hierarchy over teams, secrecy over transparency, homogeneity over diversity and conformity over risk taking?

Rob Lake made a fearless move from an overseas charity into the City. But he avoided any culture shock by positioning himself with a role and mandate that until recently was unheard of at the heart of financial institutions. Rob is head of Socially Responsible Investment at Henderson Global Investors, www.sustainablefuturefunds.com. He admits 'that my team has a different motivation from everyone else in the organization, even my boss can't quite get his head around it'. But Rob is adamant that Henderson is 'not a stiff hierarchical organization – there are City institutions that correspond to old stereotypes, but ours isn't one of them.'

researching your trip

Sightseeing is about the most exciting way of surveying what is possible. It is about dabbling in different places and cultures to experience how they really feel, taste and behave. Try temping with www.prospect-us.co.uk, a leading London recruitment agency that specializes in building careers in the 'not for profit' sector. And make the most of weekends off. The Eden Project – www.edenproject.co.uk – was so inundated with visitors it took out full-page adverts begging people not to come – might just be worth a visit then! Or you could invent your own more spontaneous day out and visit a community project like those run by www.communitylinks.org or a day shadowing a friend in a job you quite fancy. For voluntary opportunities in the UK log on to www.do-it.org.uk and www.timebank.org.uk. For experiences on the other side of the world visit www.voluntary work.org, www.vso.org.uk, www.worldwidevolunteering.org.uk, www.vol work.org.uk and www.spw.org.

Life-long learning programmes and courses are listed on www.learndirect.com, www.bbc.co.uk/learningzone, www.open.gov.uk/ dfeehome and www.crac.org.uk. To never stop learning is at the core of being un-ltd. But beware of ltd training that aims only to equip you with the skills to fulfil the ltd needs of your employer rather than drawing on your life-enriching talents and aspirations.

If you've got a niggling feeling about the multi-national that's just offered you the seemingly un-ltd position, do check out www.corporatewatch.org, www.eiris.org, www.ethicalconsumer.org and www.amnesty.org.uk/business for the low-down on what their annual report doesn't reveal. Seb Beloe, who works for corporate consultants www.sustainability.com urges you to 'trust in how important you are for the corporate community. Increasingly companies are battling with one another over employees and being able to recruit the best, most talented recent graduates. So you really are in a position to say I want to know what you are doing that has social and environ-mental impacts.' For news on graduates doing just that and for the latest opportunities, subscribe to the ethical careers magazine *YOUR FUTURE* published by the student campaign network www.peopleandplanet.org.

last minute check list

Compete on ethics

Your real market advantage comes when people trust and have faith in you. How do you plan to do that?

Think global

Although you are from . . . . there is a good chance you'll end up working somewhere else. Your desire to be a global citizen can offer un-ltd advantage.

Do the deal

Un-ltd success seems to involve negotiation. The more you can be a deal maker, the better your chances.

Be a leader, not a manager

Bureaucrats are commodities. There are lots of us who only feel able to go for safe, emotionally denying lives. Leaders are highly prized. Original thinking, good crack, hardworking, responsible, life-loving, optimistic. The good news is we are all a mixture of the two – the question is where are you heading?   ▶

Use learning as your stimulant of choice

Did anyone ever tell you your brain is a mussel? It is time to shell out on some new attitudes.

Get into the maths of entrepreneurialism

At some point, there is a business case for what you really want to do. Your current expenses — how much? Your hoped for earnings — how much? The deal maker needs some fluency with those — so consider where you stand — the numbers are often the plan to success, even more than words.

For those of you who think – dear God and I'm only 22. Please be encouraged . . .

'I do nothing but go about persuading you all, old and young alike, not to take thought for your persons or your properties, but and chiefly to care about the greatest improvement of the soul. I tell you that virtue is not given by money, but that from virtue comes money and every other good of man, public as well as private. This is my teaching, and if this is the doctrine which corrupts the youth, I am a mischievous person.'

Socrates quoted by Plato in 'The Death of Socrates'

what to visit

The un-ltd mindset refuses to define who you are by your work title. To allow a label like accountant, lawyer, cleaner, gardener or technician to count for more than the unique, exceptional person that is you, is to admit defeat to a desperately limited idea of life. How many times have you wanted to rebuff that predictable question at parties about what it is that you do? If you happen to be in one of 10 professions that a BBC poll declared as 'least respected' then that question doubly sucks.

> **To allow a label like accountant, lawyer, cleaner, gardener or technician to count for more than the unique, exceptional person that is you, is to admit defeat to a desperately limited idea of life.**

BBC poll of least desirable professions

1. Member of Parliament
2. Estate Agent
3. Government Minister
4. Lawyer
5. Journalist

▶

---

6. Footballer

7. Advertising Executive

8. Car Dealer

9. Company Director

10. Accountant

There is a poem that probably plagues your hotmail account nearly as much as those petitions to save the rainforest but here are a few lines that say something profound.

'It doesn't interest me what you do for a living. I want to know what you ache for, and if you dare to dream of meeting your heart's longing. It doesn't interest me where or what or with whom you have studied. I want to know what sustains you, from the inside, when all else falls away.'

I mean, surely you are driven to be an accountant or IT consultant for more than just the intricacies of Excel. Maybe you want to be an accountant to further a purpose and enterprise that genuinely captivates you. Whether it is for the *Big Issue* or for a medical practice or for a firm that produces really excellent products or services, you are part of something bigger and more important than just the finance team.

So let's break away from the ltd career definitions of personnel manager and PR consultant. Let's have a stab at exploring the broader ideas and prospects that characterize the brave new economy. This is not going to be comprehensive. It is simply a taste, a sampling from a world bursting with opportunities. What follows is a high-energy exposure to the websites, books and ventures that reveal opportunities and innovations that you could be part of.

business as unusual

new economics

Anita Roddick describes her values-driven, global enterprise as doing 'business as unusual'. *Take it Personally* is a coffee table anthology that Roddick edited, full of radical thought and photographs about the global economy and many of the world's most insidious corporations. For more evidence that business as usual is dying dip into David Korten's *Post-Corporate World*. The author's long-term career within the corporate establishment makes his critique especially potent.

The *Lugano Report* purports to be a secret research document on the future of the global economy commissioned by the major global powers and written by an anonymous 'working group'. A final chapter reveals that the book has a renowned but altogether different author, yet this playful twist doesn't detract from the book's sombre truths. *On the Edge* is an anthology of diverse essays, edited by Will Hutton and Anthony Giddens, that ask whether contemporary capitalism is compatible with social cohesion and justice.

Dipping into any combination of these books will help you chart the con tours of an economic system ripe for change. If these revelations stimulate you to join the architects of a new economics check out the think-tanks www.new economics.org, www.tomorrowscompany.com, www.common purpose. org.uk, www.demos.co.uk, www.theworkfoundation.com or, if working in Amsterdam excites you, www.tni.org. If all this thinking and policy is too removed from the change you'd like to orchestrate check out www.timebanks.co.uk, www.communitylinks.co.uk, www.aandb.org.uk, www.charityrecruitment.co.uk or www.justdosomething.net.

social enterprise

E F Schumacher's seminal work, *Small is Beautiful* is an international bestseller that has been an inspiration to pioneers of community enterprise. As a taste of that booming social enterprise check out CREATE, www.createuk.com, who reclaim and repair household appliances, ITMP www.itmp.co.uk in Liverpool does the same thing with IT waste and have delivered 2,500 refurbished low cost PCs to people on low incomes. Sherwood Energy Village, www.sherwoodenergy village.co.uk, is transforming a 91-acre former colliery into an eco-enterprise comprising local industry, commerce, housing, education and leisure. But for a more national perspective on the diversity and scale of social enterprise log on to www.ethical-junction.org or www.greenguideonline.com. Some cities are so rich in social enterprise that they have their own online gateways; www.coenterprise.co.uk is an insight into the social economy of Birmingham, www.sel.org.uk does the same for London. For organizations wishing to build social leadership and diversify skills, as well as project/financial management, the Magic Outcomes programme offers a schools-based programme over one year – see www.magicsandwich.co.uk. For anyone intrigued about finding social business solutions to community problems, The Cat's Pyjamas is provoking debate at dynamic training events. So do 'paws for thought' at www.the-cats-pyjamas.com.

ethical finance

Moral considerations are shaking up the nation's spending and investment habits. Research commissioned by the Cooperative Bank shows ethical purchasing growing more than six times faster than the overall economy. The value of ethical purchases grew 19 per cent from 1999 to 2000 and amounts to £13.4 billion.

Ethical finance combines financial objectives with a commitment to concerns that include social justice, economic development, peace and a healthy environment. Check out www.uksif.org, a gateway into an array of pioneers in ethical

finance as diverse as billion pound asset managers'
www.jupiteronline.co.uk and a fledgling fair-trade company
www.divinechocolate.com.

For a bible on ethical finance dip into *Morals, Markets and
Money: Ethical, Green and Socially Responsible Finance* by
Alan Lewis and published by FT Prentice Hall. For professional qualifications in social and ethical accounting, auditing and finance contact Manchester Business School
www.thencbs.co.uk, the Department of Accounting and Finance
at the University of Glasgow www.gla.ac.uk or the Social
Accountability Programme at the University of Warwick's
Business School www.wbs.warwick.ac.uk.

authentic leadership

Founder of VISA, Dee Hock, has written *Birth of the Chaordic
Age*. It is both the life story of this maverick banker and a
compelling manifesto for how future 'success will depend
less on rote and more on reason, less on the authority of the
few and more on the judgement of the many, less on
compulsion and more on motivation, less on external control
and more on internal discipline'.

To translate Dee Hock's ideas into something tangible, try
bringing different-coloured hats to the next meeting you
dread being subjected to. This is a metaphorical idea
proposed by Edward de Bono in his bestselling book *Six
Thinking Hats*. His ideas of parallel thinking involve everyone

moving in the same direction and designing 'what could be' rather than arguing over 'what is'. If you are still arguing rather than co-creating and are tired of meetings that go nowhere and of chaotic planning sessions then why not do a two-day course in facilitating a culture of participation – see www.ica-uk.org or changeactivist.com.

Peter Senge has become the guru of progressive management consultants with his book *The Fifth Discipline*. He moots the idea of a 'learning organization' based on 'systems thinking' – a corporate framework informed by the interface of science and spirituality. For more on 'systems thinking' do the progressive MBA offered by the New Academy of Business and receive an MSc in Responsibility and Business Practice, www.new-academy.co.uk.

Vacuous websites are the speciality of now countless management consultancies, but two do stand out from the crowd. Breakthrough Technologies – www.breakthrough.co.uk specializes in leadership consulting and training, and www.ideas unlimited.com are agents of change who ask uncomfortable questions but generate answers that have surprised and enlightened many of our national institutions.

sustainability consulting

Working as a consultant for some of the worst polluters and for companies not renowned for their ethical overseas working practices risks becoming complicit with practices you wanted to change. But some consider it to be the most powerful leverage point for institutional change and corporate consultants www.sustainability.com, www.accountability.org.uk and www.forumforthefuture.org.uk revel in it.

Natural Capitalism: The Next Industrial Revolution was heralded as a 'huge deal' by Bill Clinton and for another book that frames saving the planet as a 'win win' scenario for business read *Factor Four: Doubling Wealth – Halving Resource Use* for the big idea that we can live twice as well yet use half as much. For perspectives on smaller scale technology and the values of simplicity read www.resurgence.org.

The Natural Step is a science and systems-based framework used by Forum for the Future and corporate sustainability consultants around the world to develop strategic sustainability initiatives – www.naturalstep.org. *Green Futures* magazine, www.greenfutures.org.uk, and *Fast Company*, www.fastcompany.com, are the ambassadors of shiny happy ethical enterprise. *The Ecologist* magazine, which specializes in radical journalism, is not always so sympathetic – see www.theecologist.org.

redesign

efficient engineering

Cities for a Small Planet, by renowned architect Richard Rodgers of www.richardrogers.co.uk, presents novel ideas of high-density cities combining efficiency with an effective community. *Low-Tech Light-Tech High-Tech: Building in the Information Age* by Klaus Daniels explores the future of sustainable building, which is namely: integrated, high-quality, contextual, resource conserving and efficient building in which ecological assessment and planning are critical. XCO2, www.xco2.com, is a partnership between architects and structural engineers designing technologies that aid carbon dioxide reduction through energy efficiency and renewable energy.

Do a trip to the acclaimed Centre for Alternative Technology in North Wales, www.cat.org.uk, and arrive by water-powered cliff railway. Solar Century, www.solarcentury.com, is a budding solar PV solutions business with big ambitions for recruiting graduates. Log on to www.bedzed.org.uk for details of a cutting edge housing and office development who have made a low-impact lifestyle convenient and desirable; the architects responsible are at www.zedfactory.com. Also visit the Peabody Trust www.peabody.org, who play a major role in inner city regeneration.

innovative design

The Total Beauty of Sustainable Products by Edwin Datschefski
is bursting with innovations. For a taste of just how diverse
design solutions to the world's problems have become check
out wind-up radios www.freeplay.net and mail order home
products at www.naturalcollection.com. Patagonia, www.pata
gonia.com, manufacture fleece clothing from plastic bottles –
over the last decade they've diverted 40 million of them from
landfill sites into their clothing range and according to
www.dti.gov.uk there is a power station in Suffolk powered
by chicken shit. Or for more waste solutions check out
www.livingmachines.com – they are so innovative that advertising agency www.stlukes.co.uk want to install one in their
central London offices. Log on to www.bugbugs.co.uk for a
lucrative job riding those rickshaw, pedicab, cycle/taxi
things.

Design Week and *ID* are backing a graphic design manifesto
'First Things First'. It states that too much design energy is
being spent to promote consumerism and too little to helping
people understand an increasingly complex and fragile world
– there is more online at www.adbusters.org. Progressive design
agencies include www.ethicalmedia.com, www.susseddesign.com,
www.ethicalworks.com and www.wave.coop.

organic architecture

New Organic Architecture by David Pearson is a colourful portrayal of 20 architects from all over the world who have pioneered vibrant building design that is individualistic, asymmetrical and inspired by natural forms. *The New Natural House Book* is a more practical guide that examines interior elements of our living spaces spanning air, light and furniture.

Greenwich Millennium Village acts as a standard bearer not only in its architecture and design but also in its vision of how to create new, more intelligent forms of sustainable living – see www.greenwich-village.co.uk.

For a short course in creating sustainable communities visit www.findhorn.org or www.strawbalefutures.org, which isn't quite as esoteric as its sounds. For the architects and consultants behind some of the most innovative community architecture check out www.architype.co.uk, Scotland-based consultants www.thirdwave.org.uk and Cumbrian architects www.lowerae architects.co.uk. Freeform, based in Hackney, North London represent a fusion of architects and artists pioneering public art and sculpture in urban regeneration across the country – www.freeform.org.uk.

For innovative architecture and design courses and degrees explore Oxford Brookes, www.brookes.ac.uk, The Prince of Wales Institute for Architecture, www.princes-foundation.org,

Aberdeen School of Architecture, www.rgu.ac.uk, Goldsmiths College, www.goldsmiths.ac.uk, De Montfort University, www.dmu.ac.uk and for short courses www.cfsd.org.uk and www.cat.org.uk. 02 – www.o2.org – is an international network for sustainable design, www.demi.org.uk, the Royal Institute of British Architects – www.architecture.com and www.edaweb.org are indispensable if surveying opportunities for work.

open minds

free-thinking media

Manufacturing Consent by Eduard Herman and Noam Chomsky is an uncompromising critique of the elite consensus that structures the media. For some of the more free-thinking jobs in the media keep logging on to media-guardian.co.uk. Oneworld Online, www.oneworld.net, is a community of organizations working for social justice that co-ordinates world news for yahoo. *New Internationalist* www.newint.org, *ZNET* www.zmag.org and members of www.altpress.org focus attention on some of the most marginalized international stories. For a gateway into journalist training log on to www.nctj.com or to specialize in broadcast journalism try www.bjtc.org.uk.

BBC World, www.bbcworld.com, broadcasts many of the films promoted by www.tve.org and www.global-vision.org, who are catalysts for the production of progressive films. John Pilger,

pilger.carlton.com, specializes in hard-hitting investigative films on themes tackled with more humour by the Channel 4 *Mark Thomas Product*, www.mtcp.co.uk.

An exhibition of haunting but inspiring photographs from photojournalist Adian Arbib can be seen online at www.arbib.org. Panos Pictures is a photoagency representing photojournalists around the world, at www.panos.co.uk. Photovoice provide training in photography and documentary skills for refugees, streetchildren and women living with HIV around the world – www.photovoice.org hosts some of their exhibitions. Right Angle Productions in Oxford use film to help local kids take action on things they care about by making their own films – www.rapaction.org.uk. An online forum, www.comminit.com, is designed to advance partnerships between those communicating social change.

dot.com

Digital Futures: Living in a Dot.Com World, edited by James Wilsdon, brings together leading thinkers to address the future of e-commerce and offers a template for corporate responsibility in the digital age – for more information see www.digital-eu.org. If you fancy yourself as an internet entrepreneur check out the definite portal to resources you'll need at www.beyondbricks.com. An 'ethical incubator' www.drparsley.com, who has helped develop countless sustainable dot.com businesses, including the *Big Issue*, could also come in handy.

To connect with the tech and media players of the new economy go to an event hosted by www.vitamin-e.net. Check out the online market place for social change hosted by www.smartchange.org and for an Internet Service Provider geared to the needs of non-profit organizations log on to www.gn.apc.org. Two online forums, www.communities.org.uk and www.citizensonline.org.uk explore the use of new communications technologies in community change.

education

Deschooling Society is a striking critique by Ivan Illich of how schools can obstruct learning and leave students powerless. But there is some pioneering creativity within and beyond formal education that is worth getting excited about. Children's Express, www.childrens-express.org, is an out-of-school programme that uses journalism to empower young people, giving them a voice in regional and national media so that their ideas and experiences might be more accurately reflected. Centre for Curiosity and Imagination, www.centreforcuriosity.org.uk, provides hands-on exhibitions and activities that inspire playful exploration of the world. In essence it is giving children new opportunities for learning through discovery. Weekend Arts College in London, www.wac.co.uk, provides a route into performing arts careers and builds confidence, self-esteem and creative skills within young people from low-income families. Creative Arts Projects in Education, www.capeuk.org, is a pioneer of creative learning in

Leeds and Manchester and www.thenortheast.com/ss, along with www.campaign-for-learning.org.uk, are testing ideas of innovative life-long learning. MirandaNet uses multimedia to enrich life-long learning – see www.mirandanet.ac.uk.

Thomas Telford School a, secondary school in Shropshire, www.ttsonline.net, is sited in an area of socio-economic disadvantage in which educational achievement has traditionally not been high. It now stands out not only as the highest performing comprehensive in the country thanks to its innovations in the creative use of time and space and its institutional culture that makes learning integral to its own development.

Joinedupdesignforschools, championed by www.demos.co.uk, is applying the talent of leading designers in fashion, furniture and communications to the brief 'how can good design improve the quality of life in schools'. Their collaborative approach involved pupils across the country in generated projects ranging from building a treehouse inside a classroom to enlisting one of the UK's leading menswear designers to rethink the school uniform.

TeacherNet, www.teachernet.gov.uk, is a portal for government websites packed with essential teaching information and do check out www.canteach.gov.uk and the Graduate Teaching Training Agency www.gttr.ac.uk. For jobs and regular commentary log on to *The Times* Education Supplement at www.tes.co.uk or education.guardian.co.uk.

For values-driven education networks and resources contact The Development Education Association, www.dea.org.uk, Council for Environmental Education, www.cee.org.uk, The Woodcraft Folk, www.woodcraft.org.uk and WWF's education team www.wwflearning.co.uk. The National Association of Small Schools, www.smallschool.org.uk, Steiner Schools, www.steinerwaldorf.org.uk and Human Scale Education, www.hse.org.uk are at the forefront of thinking and practice for community-based education.

new frontiers

holistic science

Questions of genetics, the arms trade, militarization of space, animal experiments and problematic funding relationships hint at the ethical dilemmas inherent in a scientific career. Nobel Peace Prize Laureate, Joseph Rotblat, writes in *Physics World* that 'an ivory tower mentality was perhaps tenable in the past when a scientific finding and its practical application were well separated in time and space . . . but for scientists today to adopt an amoral attitude is immoral, because it eschews personal responsibility for the consequences of one's actions'.

Scientists for Global Responsibility, www.sgr.org.uk, have an online guide entitled 'An Ethical Career in Science and Technology?'. The Institute of Science in Society, www.i-sis.org, GeneWatch, www.genewatch.org, the International Network of Engineers, Scientists for Global Responsibility, www.inesgloba.org and the journal *Science and Engineering Ethics*, www.opragen.co.uk tackle questions on the morality of science. For a directory bursting with thousands of the most responsible and progressive institutions and scientists across Europe check out www.sd-eudb.net. *New Scientist* is the hub of recruitment for scientists and researchers – www.newscientistjobs.com.

Holistic science is a response to the limitations of dealing with isolated crises and provides instead a systems framework for the understanding of complex wholes. It is moving from a science of manipulation to one of participation in processes that are too complex to be controlled but which we can influence. The University of Plymouth and www.schumacher college.org have launched the first postgraduate programme to offer an MSc in Holistic Science.

food

BBC presenter and farmer John Humphrys has written *The Great Food Gamble*, which tackles questions of food and farming in the wake of BSE, foot and mouth and concerns of factory farming. Jose Bove, the infamous French farmer who led a protest into the town of Millau and dismantled, to cheering crowds, the new McDonald's, has written *The World is Not for Sale*. It is a stinging, amusing critique of 'malbuffe', 'horrible nosh' and the globalization of agriculture.

Three out of every four households in the UK now buy organic food, which is a testament to www.soilassociation.org, the flagship catalyst of this explosive movement. Farmers markets, in which the growers sell their produce direct to us, are springing up all over the country – see www.farmers markets.net. Planet Organic, www.planetorganic.com, and 'Out of this world', www.ootw.co.uk, are new supermarket chains dedicated to this upsurge in concern for our health and that of the planet. Hub Café in Liverpool is a more startling emblem of conscious living. It is run by Simon O'Brien, also known as Damen Grant star of *Brookside*, and not only does he pump excess solar heated water to shops on the high street, but his striking furniture is made entirely from trashed bikes.

The Royal Agriculture College in Cirencester, www.royag col.ac.uk, and Newton Rigg on the edge of the Lake District, www.newtonrigg.ac.uk, are two colleges at the forefront of agricultural innovation. For a less rigorous introduction to farming check out www.wwoof.org, particularly if you want an excuse to work on organic farms in idyllic places all over the world. For courses in sustainable land use visit www.ragmans.co.uk, a farm that produces free-range meat, cider, apple juice, honey, eggs and vegetables for hundreds of local families through a box scheme. *The Sunday Times* trumpets another box scheme, Organics Direct, for supplying vegetables at prices up to 44 per cent lower than super-markets to anywhere in the country, www.organicsdirect.co.uk.

Farms for City Children counters the poverty of experience of children from inner cities by organizing muddy weeks on country farms www.farmsforcitychildren.co.uk. And sticking out in the heart of our urban metropolis are over 1,200 city farms, www.farmgarden.org.uk, that attract 3 million visitors a year. Grab 5 is promoting fruit and vegetables to the children of low-income families – www.grab5.com. The Food Poverty Project work to improve access to healthy diets for people on low-incomes through community cafés, food-growing projects and cooking clubs – see www.food.poverty.hda online.org.uk. Carmel McConnell founded the Magic Sandwich, www.magicsandwich.co.uk, providing nutritious breakfasts to primary school children – for one in four UK kids, the only hot food they receive is provided at school.

joined up health

Joined up thinking is what the Foundation for Integrated Medicine, www.fimed.org, was set up to promote. The British Holistic Medical Association are also on the case and define 'holistic medicine' as whole person health care. Holistic practitioners aim to treat their patients or clients as whole people with psychological, spiritual, emotional and social as well as physical needs. The term 'Holistic Medicine' can include any form of health care from major surgery to acupuncture as long as it is practiced according to these principles. To aid translation of this philosophy into practice, the BHMA has defined its view of the way forward for health care in the 21st century online at www.bhma.org.

The Glasgow Homeopathic Hospital is a national centre for integrating complementary and orthodox medicine. It is housed in a brand new architectural oasis, the product of a competition that attracted the latest thinking about how design, natural light and space improves our disposition.

Liverpool's John Moores University have a centre for Health, Healing and Human Development – see www.livjm.ac.uk. They also publish *The Journal of Contemporary Health*, which is quite unlike an academic journal. It is passionate that contemporary health crises such as AIDS, BSE, cancer and smoking are not just clinical problems but require an understanding of the wider social and political processes. It does precisely that by tackling themes as diverse as community, sexuality, environment and social justice. The music therapy department at the Welsh College of Music and Drama is evidence of this multi-disciplinary approach to health, see www.wcmd.ac.uk. For more opportunities search www.nursing-courses.co.uk and the British Association of Social Workers online at www.basw.co.uk.

public interest law

McLibel by John Vidal is a gripping story of how two unemployed activists were sued by one of the world's biggest corporations. Helen, aged 19, and Dave, a single dad, printed some rather scrappy looking leaflets entitled 'What's wrong with McDonald's'. It provoked the longest-running legal saga in UK history in which the company found itself on trial. The persistent pair didn't exactly win but they did hugely embarrass McDonald's and as www.mcspotlight.org examines, the trial has lasting political and legal significance.

To join a network of lawyers, solicitors, barristers and academics working to protect civil liberties log on to www.liberty-human-rights.org.uk. As one example of how they are upholding the spirit of Human Rights Acts, Liberty has acted for some of the families of the 550 people who died in police custody since 1990.

Malcolm Lynch Solicitors provide commercial advice to players in the social economy and they publish a quarterly bulletin online at www.malcolmlynch.com. Sinclair Taylor, www.sinclairtaylor.co.uk, are driven by the same social purpose and operate from a hub in Notting Hill. EarthRights Solicitors, www.earthrights.org.uk, have been in the headlines with their High Court action against the Secretary of State of the Environment for allowing the planting of GM crops on fields adjoining one of the county's leading organic farms. *The Times*' Justice Awards heralded the Environmental Law Foundation for doing the most to widen access to justice through their work offering legal expertise to communities asserting their right to clean and safe environments – for more information visit www.elflaw.org.

getting there

To crash land into your new un-ltd work could be fatal. So how do you plan to arrive?

take a direct flight

Comfort and convenience is guaranteed. Maybe you see yourself as an executive and are impatient to start climbing. If you are really looking the part and arrive JIT (just in time) there is an outside chance you'll get upgraded. This has conventionally been the fast track route to success. But more of us than ever are doing the un-ltd thing of taking the time and space to decide what it is that we really want to do and refusing to accept that we are missing out on the career ladder in the process.

A survey of imminent graduates conducted by www.reed.co.uk revealed that only 25 per cent expect to start working immediately post graduation, while a third anticipate waiting at least nine months before starting work – allowing time for travel and discovering the perfect opportunity. Monster.co.uk claims to be the world's leading recruitment site, but for jobs with a social and ethical remit log on to jobs.oneworld.net, www.tpp.co.uk, www.charitycareers.com, www.lifeworth.com, www.ethical careers.org and society.guardian.co.uk.

do a stop over

Temp. Volunteer. Not financially rewarding in the short term but an incredible investment in the future. This is your chance to take stock of life before getting consumed in it. Make yourself indispensable to somebody or some enterprise you admire and absorb all the experiences and skills you can. Seeking short bursts of experience and insight is becoming the predominant trend – less than 50 per cent of graduates expect to stick at their first job for longer than two years.

Maybe this is a chance to open yourself up to the world. You could work in a drugs rehabilitation unit in Tower Hamlets – see www.addaction.org.uk – monitor the effects of climate change in Antarctica – www.antarctica.ac.uk – or, to pay your way, try www.overseasjobs.com.

Sometimes the reverse happens. Some of us stop over inside the system – land a well paid job with the intention of building up some security before doing something we really want to devote our lives to. Problem is, many end up cancelling the second leg of the flight because we get stuck in a catch 22 scenario, needing the corporate job just to maintain the lifestyle that goes with it.

But let me hit you with a host of people who were compelled to jump ship from their ltd career. Caroline Price made quite a leap out of her first job at the Bank of England into a radical, creative think-tank. She described the move as 'thrilling' and is now part of a team at The New Economics Foundation, which is dabbling in ventures as diverse as 'plugging the leaks' to stop money pouring out of local economies, time banks, community finance and work rethinking the global economy.

Craig Cohon was one of the top marketing executives for Coca-Cola. But while attending Davos, the ski resort that hosts an elite annual gathering of the world's movers and shakers, he decided to quite his job. He founded globalegacy – an effort to raise £100 million to fight urban poverty.

A stopover arrived for Dr Catherine Hewitt after 30 years working in a conventional medical practice. It was only at the point when her children had become independent that she had enough free time and financial security to take on the big all-consuming challenge of setting up her practice in Northampton. Her patients now include the homeless and asylum seekers.

get an around the world ticket

This is for the open minded. For the adventurous. A good move if your passion is bubbling away but you don't know exactly where to apply it. According to Rob Lake, an ethical investment advisor in the City, the best recipe 'is to experience a bit of everything, so you can understand different perspectives'. This is the strategy of dabbling in lots of places and things in the hope that one might captivate you. You could get a scholarship from www.forumforthefuture.org.uk for a 10-month placement programme with the captains of industry and come out with a Masters in Leadership for Sustainable Development. You could quite literally log on to www.cheapflights.co.uk and do some volunteering with www.spw.org.uk in Nepal and Tanzania or work with Ladakhi families for a month in the Himalayas – see www.isec.org.uk.

hitchhike

You risk missing the boat, but maybe that's the point. This is an experience with no destination. It is likely to be rich in insights and knowledge about yourself and the world. This is testing, risky stuff. It is the antithesis of landing in a ltd job. Deviating off the beaten track is the game played by entrepreneurs and by many who are self-employed.

Frank grew up in Dublin, went to art college and then a friend tempted him to move to Edinburgh. Opportunities to join graphic design companies came his way, but he let them go because they just didn't do it for him. He found himself working in a hotel and hated it, 'I had all this art and philosophy going around in my head and I was trying to serve coffee at the same time and I was just like I don't know ya – you are some business person, doing something with a laptop but I don't know what it is. I wanted to develop close links with people – but we'd just go and get trashed after work and I didn't manage to develop real links with these people and as for the customers they were here one day gone the next.' Then he had 'a crappy job doing hairdresser promotions' but with a shaved head it didn't seem to work. Then he had a stint being unemployed, his days spent doing art on his doorstep.

Frank now pioneers community arts work centred on graffiti and spray painting. It is the kind of work that is 'really agitating perception'. He started working with an arts centre in Craigmiller, the poorest area of Edinburgh. But being an outsider was a stark limitation, so he made a brave decision to apply for some pretty undesirable housing on the Estate. He moved in. It just took 'one painting up there to totally change the landscape and people's perceptions.' Kids swarmed and joined in, 'I use these interactions to say – have self-respect for your streets, have control over your environment, take self-control, compose your thoughts, get to grips with vocabulary, think about the very fabric of seeing and destiny and where you are going – this is what I talk about in graffiti.' The interest in 'my work has gone mental, I am amazed at who phones me up now to do the most varied kind of work.'

Hitchhikers juggle portfolio lives. Nina Planck was a journalist for *TIME* magazine and a speechwriter for the American ambassador in London when she started Islington Farmers Market. She borrowed a little bit of money off her boyfriend and three years later there are nine weekly farmers' markets booming all over London. But she 'adores politics' so having put in motion a national trend for reconnecting with the growers of the food we eat, she is moving back to the US in pursuit of Hillary Clinton in the hope that she might need some speeches writing.

Twenty per cent of graduates would love their first job to be abroad. While un-ltd travellers aspire after the enriching, often thrilling experiences found on the other side of the world, un-ltd thinking also confronts the confusing complexity of it all. Becky Tarbotton works in the idyllic, stark Himalayan region of Ladakh. She admits it was 'difficult working in a culture that is not my own, because ultimately you are always an outsider and even though I have learned a huge amount, I feel like there is a time limit on how long you can be away. I became confused about where I really belonged. But it has given me a commitment to find home and commit to creating change there.'

where to stay

You could choose a ltd cramped, stuffy, single-minded office. Or choose to be part of an un-ltd noisy workplace with lively conversation and workstations that embrace the flexible principles of hot-desking. Comfort, creativity and well being has become so paramount that un-ltd work spaces now resemble our living rooms.

Then again, many of them are our living rooms. With the growth of technology to support home working more freelance and female-centred enterprises and with government incentives to help reduce traffic pollution, one in seven of the UK workforce now work from home – for more information see www.wfh.co.uk. With more and more work now being done at home it begs the question, when's home time? For help contending with the blurring boundaries between work and leisure see www.dti.gov.uk/work-lifebalance.

One thing is clear, un-ltd creativity and friendship doesn't flourish anywhere near the boardroom. Julian Richer of hi-fi retailer Richer Sounds pays his staff to go to the pub, because the best ideas get generated there. J.K. Rowling wrote *Harry Potter* from inside Edinburgh coffee shops. St Lukes advertising agency, www.stlukes.co.uk, have an entirely portable phone system and use workstations that anyone can occupy at anytime.

medical kit

Half a million people in the UK suffer from work-related stress at a level that is making them ill. But insurance is rarely thrown in as part of the package deal anymore. To nurture a sense of worth and security, connect with like-minded people – for a sampling of networks that host regular events log on to www.pioneersofchange.net, www.svneurope.org, www.greendrinks.org and www.vitamin-e.net.

Even being un-ltd should carry an ample dose of health precautions. Over to our favourite pundit Jem Bendell again who admits that 'eventually my health got worse and worse, probably to do with the stress, insecurity and solitude of working freelance and the constant self-questioning associated with working within the system but not wanting to be of the system.' After six years Jem took time out to reflect and the dangers became obvious, for 'over time you can forget your original motivation and values, because you just do what you do, you also forget your life, because you seem to think you are what you do.' Evidence like this stimulated Jem to spend some of his time setting up www.lifeworth.com, which connects those working on issues of corporate social responsibility and offers a specialist head hunting service.

Once you've landed the ideal job, do you want some help keeping your ideals alive? A mentor could provide a space for you, in confidence, to reflect on how your job is developing and to discuss where you are experiencing tensions, say between your personal values and your work. It is increasingly common for employers to provide their 'high flyers' with such services, as they want those they are investing in to be able to question, develop and feel happy and confident in what they are doing. A mentoring service with a strong values base is offered by www.spaceplc.com, or you can design your own with a friend or colleague with some help from *Coach Yourself*, which is published by Momentum. Another resource is *Soultrader*, also by Momentum, to help you find the stick to you life's purpose.

If the closest you get to being appreciated in your ltd work is when you phone in sick and get soothing music tenderly interrupted with the recorded message 'you are important to us, we will be with you shortly' then it might be time to give them a shock and leave.

To stay healthy nothing beats doing the work you really love to do, for it is full of rewards that instil a sense of pleasure and fulfilment. Being un-ltd keeps you alive and motivated, for doing something you believe in passionately releases talents and capacity you didn't even know you had.

The rewards and triumphs of running a clinic for the homeless, asylum seekers, prostitutes and travellers are humbling but profound. Dr Catherine Hewitt explains:

'All our client groups are so grateful to us – because they have perceived that they are unwelcome in other practices. You see people with drug and alcohol problems stabilizing. It is small things – we're not talking magical stories like the ones in magazines where they stop using drugs and go off and save the world. But they begin to wash and they start eating better and start putting weight on and this is success – if you can see that someone is growing in self-respect and self-esteem you are making progress.'

But however fulfilling, natural disasters and wild animals can make un-ltd a dangerous place to be. Geetie and Esther are the dynamic young entrepreneurs behind three gastro pubs in London with plans for 10 more. They won *Time Out* pub of the year award 2000 and were also awarded 'businesswoman of the year'. But let's start at the beginning, for a week into the renovation work on their first pub, NatWest plc missed the plot and pulled out the start-up money they'd pledged. Esther explains that she 'was designing the kitchen when the call from NatWest came through. I had to pretend that I was having a perfectly normal conversation, the chef had just left her job to work for us and building work was well under way.' They had seven days to find the money, or the building work and their dreams would come to nothing, 'so we just went out, and manically asked everyone we knew whether they would invest, we were handing out business plans left, right and centre.' By the end of the week they'd raised the money. Esther admits 'it was quite a miracle, we were absolutely shattered, we'd put so much energy into every waking moment.'

travel literature

Bird, Polly, *Dare to be Different – 101 Unconventional Careers* (1999) Hodder & Stoughton

Bolt, Laurence, Zen and the Art of Making a Living (1999) Penguin

Bove, Jose and Dufour Francois, *The World is Not for Sale: Farmers Against Junkfood* (2002) Verso

Daniel, Klaus, *Low-Tech Light-Tech High-Tech* (2000) Birkhauser

Datchefski, Edwin, *The Total Beauty of Sustainable Products* (2001) RotoVision

Davidson, Andrew, *Smart Luck & the Seven Other Qualities of Great Entrepreneurs* (2001) Financial Times Prentice Hall

de Bono, Edward, *Six Thinking Hats* (2000) Penguin

Franks, Lynne, *The Seed Handbook – the Feminine Way to Create a Business*, (2000) HarperCollins

George, Susan, *The Lugano Report: On Preserving Capitalism in the Twenty-First Century* (1999) Pluto Press

Griffiths, Jay, *Pip Pip – a Sideways Look at Time* (2000) Flamingo

Hawken, Paul and Lovins, Amory, *Natural Capitalism: The Next Industrial Revolution* (2000) Earthscan

Herman, Edward and Chomsky, Noam, *Manufacturing Consent: The Political Economy of the Mass Media* (1995) Vintage

Hock, Dee, *Birth of the Chaordic Age* (1999) Berrett-Koehler

Hornby, Malcolm, *36 Steps to the Job You Want* (1997) Financial Times Prentice Hall

Humphreys, John, *The Great Food Gamble* (2002) Coronet

Hutton, Will and Giddens, Anthony (eds), *On the Edge: Living with Global Capitalism* (2001) Vintage

Illich, Ivan, *Deschooling Society* (1996) Marion Boyars Publishers

Jeffers, Susan, *Feel the Fear and Do it Anyway: How to Turn Your Fear and Indecision into Confidence* (1997) Rider

Korten, David, *The Post-Corporate World: Life after Capitalism* (2000) McGraw-Hill

Lewis, Alan, *Morals, Markets and Money: Ethical, Green and Socially Responsible Finance* (2002) Financial Times Prentice Hall

McAlpine, Margaret, *What Can I Do With No Degree?* (2002) Trotman & Co Ltd

McConnell, Carmel, *Change Activist: Make Big Things Happen Fast* (2002) Momentum

McConnell, Carmel, *Soultrader* (2002) Momentum

Oriah Mountain Dreamer, *The Dance* (2001) HarperCollins Paperback

Peake, Stephen (ed) *The Guardian Media Guide* 2003 (2002) Atlantic Books

Pearson, David, *The New Natural House Book* (1998) Simon & Schuster

Pearson, David, *New Organic Architecture: The Breaking Wave* (2001) Gaia Books

Roddick, Anita, *Take it Personally* (2001) HarperCollins

Rogers, Richard, *Cities for a Small Planet* (1997) Faber and Faber

Schumacher, E F, *Small is Beautiful: A Study of Economics as if People Mattered* (1993) Vintage

Senge, Peter, *The Fifth Discipline: The Art and Practice of the Learning Organization* (1993) Century

Vidal, John, Morris, Dave and Steel, Helen, *McLibel: Burger Culture Versus Counter Culture* (1997) Macmillan

von Weizacker, Ernst, Lovins, Amory and Lovins, L Hunter, *Factor Four: Doubling Wealth – Halving Resource Use: A Report to the Club of Rome* (1998) Earthscan

Williams, Nick, *The Work We Were Born to Do* (2000) Element Books

Wilsdon, James, *Digital Futures: Living in a Networked World* (2002) Earthscan

Writers' & Artists' Yearbook 2003 A & C Black

Choose life, choose a job. Choose a career. Choose a company that recklessly pollutes the planet. Choose dreaming you had everything. Choose mono this, mega that, revved-up, zipped up, no time, number ones. Choose ignorance. Choose to excuse yourself from screwing up lives in a country you've never heard of. Choose bowing your head, shutting up and giving in. But why would you want to do a thing like that?

Or choose to be different and let it be known. Choose to demand a reason and question the intent. Choose to be part of the solution. Choose community, space, simplicity. Choose sufficiency. Still desperate to go corporate? Then have the guts to interact on your own terms. Choose to take on the status quo and leave it reeling. And why on earth not?

Stories of un-ltd success are happening everywhere – in your town, all over the country, around the world. Good luck being one of them.

To join an online community of un-ltd people, for invitations to events and to benefit from a mentoring programme being offered by many of the un-ltd pioneers in this book log on to www.un-ltd.net.

Please stay in touch.

jonathan@un-ltd.net
carmel@magicsandwhich.co.uk

momentum prescription – let us help you work out which which book will suit your symptoms

Feel stuck in a rut? Something wrong and need help doing something about it?

◆ If you need tools to help making changes in your life: **coach yourself** (a good general guide to change)

◆ If you are considering dramatic career change: **snap, crackle or stop**

◆ If you need to work out what you'd like to be doing and how to get there: **be your own career consultant**

◆ If you need help making things happen and tackling the 'system' at work/in life: **change activist**

◆ If you think you want more from your life than a 'normal' career: **careers un-ltd**

Feel that you can never make decisions and you just let things 'happen'?

◆ If you need help making choices: **the big difference**

◆ If you want to feel empowered and start making things happen for yourself: **change activist**

Feel life is too complicated and overwhelming?

◆ If you need help working through office politics and complexity: **clued up**

◆ If you need a kick up the backside to get out of your commerce-induced coma: **change activist**

◆ If you need an amusing and very helpful modern life survival guide: **innervation**

◆ If you never have enough time or energy to get things done or think properly: **mental space**

Feel like you might be in the wrong job?

◆ If you want help finding your destiny job and inspiration to make that dramatic career change: **snap, crackle or stop**

◆ If you feel like you aren't doing a job that is really what you are about: **soultrader**

◆ If you are struggling with the 'do something worthwhile OR make money dilemma': **change activist**

◆ If you think you want more from your life than a 'normal' career: **careers un-ltd**

Feel that you're not the person/leader you should be?

◆ If you want to be the kind of person others want to follow: **lead yourself**

◆ If you don't feel your working relationships with people could improve: **manage yourself**

◆ If you need help becoming the person you've always wanted to be: **reinvent yourself**

◆ If you want to work out everything you've got to offer, and how to improve that: **grow your personal capital**

Feel you need help getting your ideas into action?

◆ If the problem is mainly other people, lack of time and the messiness of life: **clued up**

◆ If the problem is communicating your thinking: **hey you!**

◆ If the problem is getting things across to other people: **managing yourself**

◆ If the problem is more ideas than time and you are a bit overwhelmed with work: **mental space**

◆ If the problem is making change in your life: **coach yourself**

Feel you aren't projecting yourself and managing your career as well as you should?

◆ If you'd like to be the kind of person people think of first: **managing brand me**

◆ If you'd like people to listen to your ideas more readily: **hey you!**

◆ If you'd like to come across as the person you really are inside: **soultrader**

◆ If you need general help in changing the way you work/life: **coach yourself**

◆ If you need help working out what you've got and how best to use it: **float you**

Feel you'd like to be much more creative and a real 'ideas person'

◆ If you need inspiration on how to be innovative and think creatively: **innervation**

◆ If you need help spreading your ideas and engendering support: **hey you!**

Change Activism Where You Work

If you liked the ideas in this book, a number of workplace or personal change seminars are available based around the ideas in *Change Activist* and *Soultrader*. A brave alternative to the same old, same old.

See **changeactivist.com** for more details, or call 0207 485 7681.

The Purposeful Leader Programme

A two-day programme based on *Change Activist* and *Soultrader*. Learn
- what you really want to be when you grow up
- how to identify the fears that might be holding you back – and how to get over it
- building a trust based workplace
- social activism in your own life (media management, focus, action orientation)
- the benefits waiting when your business becomes a socially responsible business
- what makes you happy – and how to create a career based on what you really want
- feeling in control, for beginners.

Available for groups of 6–16 with individual coaching options.

Rapid Results Workshops

Two-hour facilitated event. Make big things happen fast.
Solve the problem – don't agonise act!
Can be scary. Is very effective. Not recommended for fossils.

Available for groups of 2–30

Lets Do Diversity (properly)

A half day seminar to look at the hot topic of workplace diversity and inclusion. With the change activist, without the PC guilt, business number watching or old boys club mindset. Do you want a feedback rich, genuinely trust-based workplace? This seminar gets everyone involved in that process. Expect a genuine challenge to your workplace norms.

Available for groups of 2–200

Change Activist Coaching

A professional development coach (and activist) will spend two half-day sessions with you, to help you figure out
- your career options
- your motivation
- what kind of activist might be hiding in there
- what kind of action you need to take
- with lots of handholding as you make big things happen fast.

Available to anyone who really wants to change. A nightmare if you don't.

The Magic Sandwich

The Magic Sandwich is a child poverty initiative, started by *Change Activist* author Carmel McConnell in May 2000.

Carmel was appalled to learn that many UK children go to school without breakfast and cannot learn because of hunger. She found that primary school teachers regularly had to bring in fruit from their own pocket, to help children in their classrooms.

After consultation with a number of headteachers in the London Borough of Hackney a pilot project was set up with five schools in the borough, to supply breakfast food to the children. This trial has been running successfully since September 2001, with more schools joining the scheme in September 2002. The plan is to extend food delivery and nutrition awareness into other parts of the country in 2003. Teachers report a range of benefits from Magic Sandwich support – most often that children are more settled and able to learn at the start of the school day. Your purchase of this book means that roughly 65p will go to the Magic Sandwich charity – so thank you.

Aims and Objectives:
- The Magic Sandwich aims to provide nutritious food to school children at risk of malnutrition and to raise nutrition awareness.
- To educate children, their parents and schools staff on the link between nutrition, academic performance, health and general well-being.
- To improve the learning ability of children with better nutrition.
- To raise the awareness of the effects of poor nutrition with children, their parents and school staff and to offer advice and support.
- To improve and supplement the diet of schoolchildren.
- To involve professionals from large companies to take an interest in the children and their diet, become socially aware and gain 'hands on' experience within a structured, professionally mentored development programme the profits from which will be covenanted to the Magic Sandwich.

The project welcomes input from anyone interested in supporting the academic success of primary schoolchildren. We run regular seminars involving parents, teachers, nutritionists and local business leaders. For more information on how to get involved, please contact:

The Magic Sandwich, 5b Belmont Street, London NW1 8HJ

See **www.magicsandwich.co.uk** for more information.

If you want to contribute financially to our work, we welcome cheques made payable to the Magic Sandwich to the same address. Thanks again.

Magic Outcomes – development that makes a difference

Are you a change activist?

Would you like a little help to get there?

Magic Outcomes is a leadership development programme that really makes a difference. How? Because all profits from the Magic Outcomes programme goes to support primary schools, buying food and providing nutrition awareness. This is critical, because for 1 in 4 UK children the only hot food received is at school. (Child Poverty Action Group).

How does it work?

Magic Outcomes provides skill development in a social leadership context: participants work in a professional 'change activist' context in the schools community. Typically the Magic Outcomes student spends 1 day per month on a practical, schools-based project. This is challenging. For example, how do you build trust with diverse stakeholders? Could you produce a business case for change where you work? Do you care enough about your development to go outside your comfort zone? The programme helps you do all that. And if you can be credible and trustworthy with primary school children, hard pressed teachers and parents – you can build trust with any customer anywhere.

There is real potential for joint problem solving between your organisation and the community. High performance requires leaders with both social and business vision, Magic Outcomes delivers that, and at the same time addresses child poverty.

Change Activist Training

Excellent development support is provided throughout the programme. This includes:

- Structured workshops to provide skills and knowledge development in key areas (valuing diversity, consumer trends, project leadership, gaining action muscle).
- One-to-one mentoring (with experienced public and private sector mentors).
- Knowledge to help you understand how the public and voluntary sector operates.
- Help to explore a range of socially fulfilling career options.
- Business measures to ensure skills are transferred back to the workplace.

If you would like to gain leadership skills, and make a difference, get in touch at **info@magicsandwich.co.uk** or call 0207 485 7681.

This is how to create leadership skills and social responsibility in the same programme. We'd love to get your change activism into action.